FINANCIAL FREEDOM FOR OTs

A Guide to Building Wealth Without Burnout

Doug Vestal, Ph.D.

Copyright © 2025 by Doug Vestal, PhD

All rights reserved.

No portion of this book may be reproduced in any form without written permission from the publisher or author, except as permitted by U.S. copyright law.

This publication is designed to provide accurate and authoritative information in regard to the subject matter covered. It is sold with the understanding that neither the author nor the publisher is engaged in rendering legal, investment, accounting or other professional services. While the publisher and author have used their best efforts in preparing this book, they make no representations or warranties with respect to the accuracy or completeness of the contents of this book and specifically disclaim any implied warranties of merchantability or fitness for a particular purpose. No warranty may be created or extended by sales representatives or written sales materials. The advice and strategies contained herein may not be suitable for your situation. You should consult with a professional when appropriate. Neither the publisher nor the author shall be liable for any loss of profit or any other commercial damages, including but not limited to special, incidental, consequential, personal, or other damages.

Book Cover by Novella Editorial

First edition 2025

Unlock Your Exclusive Resources Before You Dive In

You are going to learn in these pages just how important money mindset is as an OT.

Just to say thanks for reading this book, I'd like to give you the money mindset training that I teach inside my course "Private Pay MBA."

Go To: *www.freedomofpractice.com/money*

Here's what you've receive:

- Conquer your invisible money scripts (most OTs don't even know they have this!)
- Rewrite limiting beliefs on your thoughts about money
- Accelerate your path to financial freedom

Join a Free Community of OTs as You Read This Book

I created a Facebook group called "OT Financial Wellness" so that you have a space to discuss personal finance topics, hear from other OTs, find support and resources.

You'll discover even more OT personal finance strategies, hear what's working for other OTs, and be able to get your burning personal finance questions answered.

Praise for *Financial Freedom for OTs*

"Money underlies all of our ADLs and iADLs. So, if we want to meet our ideal of holistically problem-solving with our clients, we need to become more financially savvy. And, this begins with YOUR OWN finances. Thank you to Doug, for showing us the way."

Sarah Lyon, OTR/L, CEO OT Potential

"This book is exceptional! It is going to be the primary textbook for my Leadership and Management course. Doug does an amazing job of taking intimidating financial concepts and teaching them in a not only digestible, but enjoyable way. The skills developed through reading this book can change the life trajectory for occupational therapy professionals and students. This book covers the financial concepts everyone should understand, but all of the information is tailored to the occupational therapy provider. It is the comprehensive financial resource that all occupational therapy students and professionals need!"

Ashley Hobson, DSc, MOT, OTR/L Assistant Professor and Doctoral Capstone Coordinator at the University of Oklahoma Health Sciences

"This book is a quick and easy read, yet it delivers invaluable insights that I wish I had learned early on. It provides financial knowledge tailored for both current and aspiring OTPs, making it an essential resource for anyone beginning their OT journey or anyone striving for long-term financial stability."

Zesarae Bodie, OTD, MPH, OTR/L, Assistant Professor, Division of Occupational Therapy, Medical University of South Carolina

"Dr. Vestal presents an extraordinary and succinct roadmap for financial management and freedom from debt. He addresses his efforts specifically to occupational therapists (OTs) and their unique perspective since much of the OT's focus relates to activities of daily living, of which money management is a big part. Dr. Vestal's theories on management for financial independence, analysis of income and expenses, setting goals for improvement in each of these areas and executing those goals apply to anyone interested in financial freedom."

Judith C. Vestal (no relation to the author), PhD, OTR, Associate Professor (Retired) Louisiana State University Health Sciences Center, Shreveport, LA

"OT students spend years learning to help others live meaningful lives—yet they often graduate unprepared for their financial future. We must do better. Financial *Freedom for OTs* delivers this crucial knowledge through an OT lens, showing how financial well-being creates the stability, freedom, and choices needed to thrive in this profession. This is the education future therapists deserve."

Stacey Huffman-Main, OTD, Assistant Professor of Occupational Therapy, Drake University, Des Moines, IA

"This book offers OTs a thoughtful approach to financial independence. It beautifully connects the skills necessary for financial well-being to our amazing OT skill set, and is valuable for students, new grads, and experienced practitioners alike. This book takes the confusion out of an intimidating topic, empowering therapists to thrive both professionally and financially."

Sarah S. Sidar, PP-OTD, OTR/L, BCB-PMD, Assistant Professor, Division of Occupational Therapy, Shenandoah University

"This book is a transformative resource for occupational therapy practitioners (OTP) who want to enhance their financial management skills. Doug brilliantly unpacks deep-rooted money behaviors using a trauma-informed care approach while delivering simple, actionable strategies to build lasting wealth. Practical and refreshingly straightforward, this book is the blueprint for financial security. It equips OTPs and anyone to make intentional, sustainable money decisions, prioritizing their present and future professional and personal well-being."

Pamela Hess, OTD, OTR, DipACLM, PMH-C, Clinical Assistant Professor, Department of Occupational Therapy, College of Public Health and Health Profession University of Florida

"*Financial Freedom for OTs* is not just a book—it's a blueprint for empowerment, showing occupational therapists how to take control of their finances, build wealth, and create a career that aligns with their values and aspirations."

Tina M. Sauber, OTD, OTR/L, BCPR

"Being an OT we focus time educating our patients on health literacy and yet no where in my education was I offered knowledge on financial literacy. Financial Management is an occupation and managing student loan debt is an important aspect of financial literacy. Doug's book on Financial Freedom for OT's provides the reader with knowledge, and application. I appreciate his honesty, his stories and perseverance to tackling student loan debt. His perspectives on OT compensation is a huge driving factor into me pursuing private practice. Doug has been a wonderful mentor and I know how much this resource will greatly benefit occupational therapy students, educators and practitioners."

Danielle LeBeau MS, OTR/L Faculty and Academic Fieldwork Coordinator at Maria College

"This guide book was such a joy to read and provided easy application tools to help OTs to gain confidence in the pursuit of financial freedom! The information is valuable to all OTs from their first year of practice to 20+ years in the profession. I know as a single parent myself, I found several financial tools that I can apply today in my own life"

Sarah McCadden, OTD, OTR/L, Assistant Professor, Doctor of Occupational Therapy Program, Mary Baldwin University

"Doug gives us OTPs a lesson in one of our own ADLs - Money Management. He provides no-nonsense advice on how to excel at this ADL. His book provides excellent examples and strategies for improving wealth. Nicely, his book is catered to OTPs and the way we think about our work and managing our money. All OT programs should consider this text for their students and faculty. Thanks, Doug!"

Gina L. Pifer, EdD, OTR/L, BCPR, Associate Clinical Professor, Department of Occupational Therapy, University of Missouri

"As OTs, we're experts at helping others reach their goals -- but do we even know our own long-term financial goals? This book is your guide to gaining clarity, setting specific goals that align with your values, and taking actionable steps toward financial freedom. Whether you're an OT student entering the field or a seasoned practitioner facing financial stress, this book is for you!"

Amanda Satcher, OTD, OTR/L, C/PAM, Assistant Professor, Department of Occupational Therapy, Belmont University

"Doug successfully reframes money mindset and financial habits through the lens of our profession—using language we understand and examples that resonate. With relatable insights and practical exercises, he transforms daunting financial concepts into clear, actionable steps. Conversational and engaging, this book feels like learning from a trusted friend. A must read for occupational therapy professionals looking to build confidence, reframe their relationship with money, and create lasting financial well-being."

Carlin Reaume, OTD, OTR/L, Assistant Professor, Department of Occupational Therapy, University of the Pacific

"Wow—this book was the wake-up call I didn't know I needed! I wish someone had handed me this 25 years ago when I started as an OT. Instead of regret, I feel empowered to take control of my finances now. I never realized how taboo money was for me or how much discomfort it caused—until now. I deserve to pay myself first. I'm buying a copy for my daughter so she can start her life off right!"

Frederica O'Donnell, OTD, OTR/L

"ATTENTION! Are you an occupational therapy practitioner interested in taking control of your finances and achieving financial independence, all while maintaining a healthy work-life balance? Well, this book is for you! Reading Financial Freedom for OTs: A Guide to Building Wealth Without Burnout is approachable and pragmatic, offering actionable steps tailored specifically to OT practitioners. By framing financial management as an ADL, Doug draws a relatable parallel that makes historically intimidating content easy to digest. The strategies for student loan repayment, budgeting, and investing are clear, practical, and empowering. His advice on building wealth through compound interest and leveraging professional skills outside of traditional clinical roles is particularly insightful. This is a fantastic resource for OT practitioners at any stage of their career looking to enhance financial well-being without compromising their passion for patient care."

Jenn Workman, OTD, OTR/L Instructor and Academic Fieldwork Coordinator, OTA Program, Cape Fear Community College

"Caring professions, like occupational therapy, require a significant financial commitment to higher education and graduate school. This book provides invaluable information that can help the seasoned practitioner, early career practitioner, and students a plan to freedom from the burdens of debt. Doug does a fantastic job of balancing information with action, keeping the reader engaged throughout the book. This is a must read for any OT looking to improve their finances."

Kandy Salter, OTD, OTR/L, CAPS, Program Director, Assistant Professor, Occupational Therapy Doctoral Program, University of Arkansas/University of Arkansas for Medical Sciences

"This book was fantastic. It was able to take difficult financial concepts and make them easily understandable, all the while weaving in OT language and values. I wish this book was around 13 years ago when I entered into practice. I will definitely be recommending this to every one of my OTS as well as co-workers and friends in the field."

Hilary Sauder, OTD, OTR/L, Academic Fieldwork Coordinator Clinical Assistant Professor Master of Occupational Therapy Program, Idaho State University

"Financial Freedom for OTs is an insightful and much-needed resource for occupational therapists seeking financial security. Doug Vestal brilliantly bridges the gap between personal finance and the distinct professional realities of being an occupational therapist, offering actionable and practical strategies to achieve financial independence without sacrificing well-being. One of many standout tools in Doug's book is his explanation of finding one's "Freedom Number", a truly innovative mindset shift for any hardworking professional. This book is particularly relevant given the rising concerns around student debt, job burnout, and financial instability within the healthcare industry. A must-read for any OT looking to gain financial independence while sustaining professional fulfillment!"

Heidi Ana Carpenter, OTD, OTR/L, MLS, RYT, Assistant Professor, Doctorate of Occupational Therapy, Huntington University Arizona

"This book is an indispensable resource for any OT entrepreneur. Doug's personable writing, combined with his wealth of experience in finance and business, makes complex concepts accessible and applicable to our field of OT. The actionable steps outlined in the book have empowered me to take charge of my financial journey and move toward the wealth and freedom I've always dreamed of. This book is a game-changer for any OT practitioner looking to level up in both their career and financial life!"

Dr. Quiara Smith, OTD, OTR/L, CEIM, Assistant Professor, Occupational Therapy Doctorate Program, Duke University School of Medicine

"This is an excellent resource for anyone hoping to gain control over their financial planning, but the way it is targeted, especially for OTs, makes it much more engaging and easy to read. It is like the author is speaking directly to me. The language is easy to understand for anyone without a financial background, and the planning activities make it that much more customizable to individual needs. I highly recommend this to every future OT/OTA or any practitioner who has not yet paid off their student loans."

Scott Hutchison, OTD, OTR/L, Assistant Professor, Medical University of South Carolina

"I'm excited to finally have a concrete, effective plan to help not only keep occupational therapy professionals in the field, but also recruit the next generation of life changers. Occupational therapy has been the best decision I've ever made—but after 20 years of insurance reimbursement battles, regulatory restrictions, student loans, I find myself asking: Did I choose a profession I could retire from? And during my tenure as AOTA President, I heard from so many in our community that are asking the same question.

Doug takes us beyond theory into practice, redefining financial security as an essential ADL in language that fits seamlessly into the Occupational Therapy Practice Framework. He applies our own mindfulness techniques to strip away the shame and guilt tied to 'money talk' and empowers OT professionals to achieve financial freedom with clarity and confidence. This book reads like an OT manual, yet it breaks down the long-standing taboo of discussing money and prepares us for success from day one in the field.

If you are even considering a career in occupational therapy, read this book. It will free you from financial trauma and have you rating wealth as one of the occupations in which you feel successful on all of your occupational profiles!"

Alyson D. Stover. MOT, JD, OTR/L, BCP
Founder & COO, Capable Kids
Associate Professor, University of Pittsburgh,
Department of Occupational Therapy
Served as President of AOTA 2022 – 2025

DEDICATION

This book is dedicated to my amazing, late Grandfather William Vestal, a former Marine who served in WWII.

I spent my senior year of high school living with my grandfather and a few summers during undergraduate school and this experience had a profound impact on me.

My grandmother suffered from debilitating rheumatoid arthritis and was wheelchair bound from the time I was a kid. My grandfather was my grandmother's primary caregiver until the day she passed away.

When I was living with my granddad I saw him wake up each day, lift my grandmother out of bed into her wheelchair (with a Hoyer lift), get her dressed, comb her hair, brush her teeth and bring her out to the kitchen and living room. He'd feed her and take care of her toileting. They'd talk about the news and he'd cook her favorite recipes. Each night he'd repeat his morning activities but in reverse.

He did this for decades with a smile on his face. He loved caring for the love of his life.

I learned a lot about what it means to care for those most important to you by watching my grandfather.

As I progressed through undergrad school, it was my grandfather who was the first to encourage me to get my Master's and Ph.D. At the time, he saw something in me that I couldn't see in myself.

My grandmother got progressively worse and eventually needed to be tube-fed. When my grandfather himself was hospitalized, it was my brothers and I who took over caring for our grandmother.

One day, my girlfriend Lindsey joined me. I'd find out later that Lindsey saw me back in my grandmother's room helping get her ready and the thought crossed Lindsey's mind of, "this is the man I'm going to marry."

While my grandfather passed away over 15 years ago, he was the best man at Lindsey and I's wedding.

I have no doubt it is the lessons I learned from my grandfather that made her want to marry me. And we are still going strong 20 years later.

I'll be forever grateful for the lessons my grandfather taught me about personal responsibility, caring for your family and how to be a good husband.

NOTES FOR THE READER

A note on the language of this book

I use the term Occupational Therapist (and OT) in this book instead of Occupational Therapist Practitioner (OTP) to save on space and wordiness. Please know that this material 100% applies to Occupational Therapy Assistants (OTAs) and this book was written with you in mind as well.

A note on the content of this book

In this book you'll see that I reference contribution limits to 401(k)'s, Roth IRAs, etc. throughout the book and in examples. This book was originally published in 2025 so these amounts reflect what is allowed in that year. However, each year the contribution limits normally change due to inflation and other economic variables. Don't worry, the concepts are still exactly the same even if the amounts change slightly from year to year. To find the most up to date contribution limits after 2025 I recommend you Google the phrase "IRS contribution limits (type of account) in (year)." So, for instance you'd Google "IRS contribution limits Roth IRA in 2027."

The information in this book about federal Income-Driven Repayment (IDR) plans, loan forgiveness programs, and other student loan policies is based on the latest available details at the time of writing. However, federal student loan programs are subject to change due to new legislation, executive actions, or policy updates from the U.S. Department of Education.

To ensure you have the most current and accurate information, I strongly recommend visiting StudentAid.gov—the official website of the U.S. Department of Education.

This book is designed to provide accurate and authoritative information on the subject of personal finance. It is sold with the understanding that neither the Author nor the Publisher or Editor is engaged in rendering legal, accounting, or other professional services by publishing this book. As each individual situation is unique, questions relevant to personal finance and specific to the individual should be addressed to an appropriate professional to ensure that the situation has been evaluated carefully and appropriately. The Author and Publisher and Editor specifically disclaim any liability, loss, or risk which is incurred as a consequence, directly or indirectly, of the use and application of any of the contents of this work.

TABLE OF CONTENTS

INTRODUCTION	**1**
Good News for OTs!	3
Why I'm Passionate About Helping OTs Build Wealth	4
Redefining Wealth for OTs	8
Your Freedom Number: The Key to Intentional Wealth-Building	10
How To Reach Your Freedom Number: The Magic of Compound Interest	19
CHAPTER ONE. THE BIG SQUEEZE FOR OTs AND WHY MONEY IS AN ESSENTIAL ADL	**25**
Money is an Essential ADL	26
Maslow's Hierarchy of Needs: The Hidden Role of Money	27
The Vicious Cycle of High Debt + Low Salary	28
The Twin Titans Threatening Your Financial Future	28
The Harsh Reality of OT Compensation	29
The Impact of Financial Stress on Professional Performance and Well-Being	33

How Money Worries Sabotage Your OT Career	33
The Silent Epidemic Affecting OTs Everywhere	34
Escaping the Financial Trap: Your Path to Abundance	36

CHAPTER TWO. OVERCOMING FINANCIAL TRAUMA: INNER WORK FOR OTs — 39

Examining Your Money Trauma	40
The Under-Earners, Under-Savers, and Under-Accumulators	45
Money: A Tool for Magnifying Your Impact	46
Examining Limiting Money Beliefs	47

CHAPTER THREE. SECRETS TO WEALTH ACCUMULATION: TAILORED ADVICE FOR OTs — 57

Forget Everything You Think You Know About Becoming Wealthy	57
Shattering the Millionaire Myth: Surprising Facts About the Wealthy	59
The Invisible Wealth: It's What You Don't Spend That Counts	60
Stop Consuming and Start Owning	61
Redefining Retirement: It's a Number, Not an Age	64

Designing Your Life on Your Terms:
Aligning Priorities and Actions   66

Becoming the "Strange" Millionaire:
Bucking Conventional Wisdom   71

Reclaiming Your Financial Independence,
Flexibility, and Freedom   72

CHAPTER FOUR. START INVESTING NOW - NOT LATER 74

Start Building Your Investing Muscle Today   75

The Just Right Challenge: Your
Four-Account Investing Roadmap   76

401(k): The Powerhouse of Your
Retirement Portfolio   77

The Employer Match: Your Golden
Ticket to Wealth   79

HSA: The Triple Tax Advantage
for Your Health and Wealth   81

Roth IRA: The Tax-Free Growth and
Withdrawal Advantage   83

Brokerage Account: Your Flexible
Investing Option   84

CHAPTER FIVE. BUILDING WEALTH FROM WHAT YOU ALREADY MAKE 86

Reframing Your Earning Potential:
An OT's Lifelong Journey   87

Designing Your Financial Roadmap:
Goal-Directed Money Management ... 88

Mindfully Examining Your
Spending Patterns ... 98

Prioritizing Your Financial Well-Being:
Paying Yourself First With a 50-30-20 Plan ... 100

Evaluating Your Financial Health:
A Holistic Assessment ... 103

Assessing Your Cashflow
and Developing a Plan ... 104

Charting Your Course to Financial
Freedom: An OT's Action Plan ... 108

CHAPTER SIX. THE DEBT TRAP: UNDERSTANDING THE TRUE COST OF BORROWED MONEY ... 110

OTs Beware: How Monthly Payments
Keep You Stressed and Broke ... 111

Uncovering the Hidden Costs of Financing ... 113

The Price of Debt for OTs: The Staggering
Cost of Debt-Fueled Spending ... 115

Drowning in Debt: Why OTs Struggle
to Get Ahead Financially ... 116

Navigating the Debt Landscape:
From Secured Loans to Sky-High Interest ... 117

The Hierarchy of Debt for OTs:
Ranking Loans from Best to Worst ... 118

The Great Debate for OTs: Is There
Such a Thing as "Good" Debt? ... 119

OT Student Loans: The Double-Edged
Sword of Financing Your Future   121

Escaping the Debt Trap: Proven Strategies for
OTs to Accelerate Their Journey to Freedom   122

Understand Your Current Debt Situation   123

Avalanche vs Snowball: Choosing Your
Path to Pay Off Your OT Debt   126

From Overwhelmed to In Control: Crafting
Your Personalized OT Debt-Freedom Plan   130

Trimming the Fat: How OTs Can Slash
Expenses to Supercharge Debt Repayment   132

CHAPTER SEVEN. PAYING OFF YOUR OT STUDENT LOANS QUICKLY: A STEP-BY-STEP GUIDE   142

Subsidized Versus Unsubsidized Loans   143

Private Loans Versus Federal Loans   146

Unraveling the Mystery of Private Loans:
Your Key to Informed Borrowing   150

Decoding Federal Loans: Navigating the
Alphabet Soup of Repayment Options   150

Slash Your Monthly Payments with These
Game-Changing Federal Programs   151

SAVE: The Insider's Guide to the Pros,
Cons, and Everything in Between   157

PSLF: Is This Loan Forgiveness
Program Right for You?   163

What's the Deal with Consolidation
and Refinancing? 169

Accelerate Your Journey to Debt Freedom:
Proven Tactics to Pay Off Your Loans Faster 170

CHAPTER EIGHT. INVESTING 101: WHAT EVERY OT SEEKING FINANCIAL FREEDOM SHOULD KNOW 178

Mastering the Building Blocks of
Investing: Assets and Accounts 180

Navigating the Investment Account Maze:
Your Key to Financial Success 183

Debunking Investment Myths:
Empowering OTs to Take Control 192

Unlocking the Secrets of Wealth:
Investment Wisdom for OTs 198

The Hidden Costs Draining
Your Investment Potential 199

The Zen of Passive Investing:
Simplicity Breeds Success 200

The Marathon Mindset:
Embracing Long-Term Investing 201

The Patient Investor:
Mastering the Buy and Hold Strategy 202

Diversification: Your Financial Safety Net 203

From Theory to Practice:
Kickstarting Your Investment Journey 206

Empowering OTs to Invest with Confidence 211

CHAPTER NINE. INCREASE YOUR INCOME AND PERSONAL SATISFACTION WITH "THE SWEET SPOT PRACTICE" — 212

    The Undeniable Truth: OTs are Vastly Underpaid — 212

    Introducing the Sweet Spot Practice: Your Key to Balance and Prosperity — 213

    Breaking Free from Insurance Constraints — 215

    You Deserve It and Your Clients Will Thank You — 217

    Serving with Intention: Overcoming Guilt and Defining Your Impact — 219

    Ideal Clients Are Willing to Invest in Results — 221

    Supercharging Your Retirement: The Owner's Advantage — 223

    Crunching the Numbers: Employees vs. Practice Owners — 229

    Sweet Spot Practices are Surprisingly Easy to Start — 230

    The Main Limiting Belief Holding OTs Back From Starting Private Pay Practices — 232

    The Five Must-Haves When Starting a Private Pay Practice — 237

CONCLUSION	245
ACKNOWLEDGEMENTS	247
Imagine Seeing 20 Clients/Week and Still Earning a Full-Time Income	249
ABOUT THE AUTHOR	250

INTRODUCTION

"Your personal experiences with money make up maybe 0.0000001% of what's happened in the world, but maybe 80% of how you think the world works."

- The Psychology of Money by Morgan House

You likely got into the OT world because you have a deep desire to help people. In graduate school, you probably found yourself looking around your classmates and your professors with the feeling: *I've found my place, my people—this is what I was meant to do.*

You learned about all the incredibly creative ways you can help people. All the amazing opportunities to transform your clients' lives.

Along the way, perhaps you took out the maximum amount of student loans for OT school because you thought: *Hey, being an OT is in-demand, and I'll always be able to find a good job.*

Once you started working, though, reality set in. Your dream became a struggle when you graduated and started a job where you had to see twelve to fifteen clients a day, plus the endless hours spent documenting.

You probably found yourself being paid less than you had expected, given all of your experience, credentials and ability to positively impact your client's lives. And those hefty student loans you took out? Well, they have started to feel like an albatross around your neck.

You've probably heard that you should be saving for retirement, but that seems impossible now due to your salary, student loan payments, and competing priorities, like starting or expanding your family or reducing your work to part-time to care for a loved one. Or simply take a vacation guilt-free.

You may not realize it, but money stress is starting to control your life.

Fighting with your spouse about whether you can afford the down payment on your dream house—that's money stress.

Feeling anxious about going part-time so you can volunteer at your kids' school, be class-parent, or take Fridays off to chaperone your kids to the museum—that's money stress.

Feeling frustrated in a job with super high productivity standards and a DOR who seems to have forgotten what it was like seeing clients all due to needing to make the minimum payments on your student loans—that's money stress.

Good News for OTs!

The topic of personal finance is a field in which almost no one ever gets a formal education. Even if you got an MBA, or an accounting degree, or a finance degree, the likelihood that you would have learned in-depth about personal finance specifically is close to 0%. Instead, personal finance is something you embark on yourself.

The famous motivational speaker Jim Rohn once said: "Formal education will make you a living; self-education will make you a fortune." And this is totally true of learning personal finance as an OT.

It may seem like a stretch right now, but there is absolutely no reason why, as an OT, you cannot become wealthy. There is no reason, as an OT, that you can't retire with millions of dollars saved and invested. There is no reason, as an OT, that you can't get a handle on your money, pay off your student loans in record time, save for retirement, *and* have the freedom and flexibility you desire.

This book will show you how by focusing on three actionable steps:

1. How you make your money
1. How you save your money
2. How you invest your money

The path to financial freedom and wealth as an OT boils down to three proactive actions: earn it, save it, and invest it. These are simple to say, but difficult to do.

This is because most personal finance advice doesn't adequately tackle the unique situation and field of OTs.

But I do in this book, which is written specifically for:

- The OT who is heart-centered but weighed down by student loans;
- The OT who loves their field but wants freedom and flexibility in their life;
- The OT who didn't get into this field for the money but now realizes that without it they can never retire;
- The OT who feels greedy thinking about money but secretly feels stuck by their career;
- The OT who feels like they are treading water and wants more abundance in their life.

Why I'm Passionate About Helping OTs Build Wealth

At the age of 17, I became intensely interested in personal finance after seeing my father mismanage his money. He had a good job. He drove a nice car. We lived in a good neighborhood. From the outside, things seemed normal.

When we went out to eat, his credit card would often get declined. He avoided answering the phone because it was frequently a collection agency.

He and my stepmother would fight like cats and dogs about their spending.

It came to a head one day when he sat me down and told me that the money he had promised to set aside for my college was gone. He had spent it. I was about to enroll in Georgia Tech, an out-of-state school. Those dreams came crashing down when I realized how much in student loans I'd have to take out to cover tuition. Instead, I enrolled in an in-state school with much lower tuition and took out a more reasonable amount of student loans.

I couldn't figure it out. My dad was smart, and I thought he was successful. When I was a kid, he seemed to have it all together. When you're a kid, though, you usually think the adults around you have it all figured out. How could he, as an adult, have messed up his money situation so badly?

This set off an intense study of money for me. I read every personal finance book I could find. I ultimately ended up getting a Master's in Financial Mathematics and then a Ph.D. in Applied Probability, focusing on a type of financial products that hedge funds traded in.

That subsequently led to a 15-year career on Wall Street. I worked for 12 years in NYC and 3 years in Paris. I managed a global team in NYC, London, and Hong Kong. But, unlike what you see portrayed in the media, my job on Wall Street was all about risk management, not the chest-beating bravado of a "boys club."

My wife graduated from OT school in 2011 from NYU. Like most NYC graduates, she graduated with about $150,000 of student loan debt. The monthly payment was close to $800/month.

In 2012, we had our first child, and then in 2014 our second child. And here we found ourselves in an all-too-familiar "OT Pickle." With two kids under age five, we needed to place both in daycare. Daycare for two kids + student loan repayments equaled my wife's entire OT salary.

Each month, we treaded water. This was the conundrum: earn money to pay for student loans, miss out on seeing our kids, and then don't have anything extra at the end of the month after all of our hard work and sacrifice.

This situation lasted about a year before we realized that this was a crazy way to live.

Sure, this is the common situation that many people find themselves in. But we realized that if we wanted the situation to change, we had to change.

Relying on all the personal finance knowledge I had and my business career, we put a plan in place to achieve more freedom. We focused on saving more, earning more, and investing more.

Following this pivot, we paid off all the student loans in three years. We accelerated our savings, which I discuss in Chapter 5. We started our own OT private pay practice, increasing our earnings, which I talk about in Chapter 9. And we turbo-charged our investments, which will be covered in Chapter 8.

Now, we are 100% debt-free. I retired from Wall Street, and we have two OT-related businesses that we run together. We are financially independent, take summers off to spend with our kids, and have the ability to live anywhere we want.

But this didn't happen overnight. It literally took decades. Building financial security is never a "quick fix" despite what you may see on social media. As you'll discover in the rest of this book, building wealth is like building a snowball. It starts off very small but then it really starts to accumulate. In later chapters I'll debunk most of the myths you probably have around what it takes to become financially independent. Your current OT salary and what you do with it for the next 10, 20 or 30 years will be enough for you to pay off your student loans, save for retirement and become financially independent.

Redefining Wealth for OTs

Money in our society is complicated. Aside from sex, I can't think of a topic that is more laden with guilt, shame, misunderstanding, desire, intrigue, and jealousy.

As a society, we don't talk openly about how much we earn. We don't talk openly about how much we spend. We don't talk openly about how much we save and invest.

Let's quickly do this exercise. Close your eyes and imagine someone wealthy. What do you see?

Most likely, you saw someone who is:

- Well-dressed, perhaps wearing a lot of jewelry or a designer suit
- Surrounded by luxury items such as expensive cars or a big house
- In an exotic location, like a secluded island
- Busy and stressed, because to be wealthy means they are constantly working
- Of questionable ethics, such as ruthless CEOs convicted of fraud or of cutting corners

These are the ways in which popular media conveys wealth in our society. Wealthy people are either matcrialistic consumers or have low moral standards—often, a toxic combination of both.

In the face of this, why would an OT want to be wealthy? Why would an OT think they could become wealthy if they don't have a CEO's salary or a celebrity's paycheck?

We need a different definition of wealthy, one that isn't focused on the external signs or focused on material consumption. To me, a wealthy OT is one who:

- Can comfortably afford to take six months off to find a new OT job instead of sticking with the one that is causing burnout.
- Can drop down to working three days a week to pursue something meaningful to them, such as starting a business, caring for loved ones, etc., and still be on track to retire.
- Can sleep well at night without money stress impacting them.
- Can make life's biggest decisions—like moving across the country, starting a family, or taking a sabbatical—based on their values and dreams, not financial constraints.
- Can pivot their career or explore new opportunities without fear—whether that's taking a passion project full-time, pursuing additional education, or transitioning into a completely different field.

The true sign of wealth is freedom and flexibility in your choices. While this may not be your reality today, it can be your reality tomorrow with the right planning. And it starts with understanding a key metric: your freedom number.

Your Freedom Number: The Key to Intentional Wealth-Building

Building wealth is difficult partially because it's often discussed in vague terms. And most people never actually sit down and define how much money they actually need.

Trying to save and invest without an end goal in mind doesn't work. It is like going on a long car trip without GPS. You won't reach your destination. And if, by some chance, you do make it, it will likely be after countless detours, setbacks, and unnecessary stress.

That all ends today. Today you are going to calculate your Freedom Number. This is probably the most important section in this entire book. Just calculating your Freedom Number will put you miles ahead of those who don't take the time to do it, so that they have no idea what destination they want to go to nor how to get there.

What exactly is your Freedom Number? Your Freedom Number is simply how much money you need to have saved to never work another day. Work becomes a choice, not an obligation. That is, your Freedom Number will allow you to cover your living expenses without relying on a paycheck by simply taking money each month from the earnings of your investments (I'll show you how to safely withdraw from your investment portfolio so you don't run out of money).

The first step is to define how much money you want to spend each month. Notice I say "want to" rather than "currently do." This is a deliberate distinction. Living in financial independence is all about living intentionally. It involves intentionally designing how you want to spend your time and the money required to go along with it.

Often, you'll have current expenses that will be eliminated by the time you become financially independent. For instance, if you are currently paying for daycare, that expense may not be there by the time you are financially independent. I would argue the same goes for both your housing and car payments. By the time you become financially independent, I want you to be mortgage-free and to buy your cars with cash.

The first step is to get specific around what you will want to do when work becomes a choice rather than an obligation. How are you spending your time? Are you traveling a lot? What hobbies are you pursuing? Do you prioritize your health and spend money on personal trainers? Do you enjoy trying new restaurants and want to be able to go out weekly with your friends without paying attention to the bill?

Only *you* can answer these questions. And the first step is to create a brief description of what your life will look like. Get super specific on how you will spend your time. Use highly charged, vivid, and powerful verbs to define your future.

The key is to avoid judging yourself while you are doing this exercise. Once you start judging your response, you'll start to change what you truly want. Imagine your life is like a movie and you are the documentarian who is transcribing what they see.

Here is an example to help you get started:

> *When work becomes a choice rather than an obligation I will live in a paid-for house. My cars will be fully paid for. I shop for organic food and take time and pride in preparing healthy meals at home. I wake up leisurely in the morning and sip french press coffee on my front porch while I read my favorite novel. After a healthy breakfast, I head off to volunteer for a couple of hours. In the afternoon I go workout at my local rec center so that I stay strong and fit. In the evening my spouse and I ride our bikes downtown where we talk over a craft beer. On the weekend, I get together each Sunday for brunch with my friends after a morning hike followed by a movie. During the summer, I travel for eight weeks to places like Italy, Croatia, and Belize. During these trips, I splurge during these trips and don't have to pinch pennies. By this point, my kids are grown and living in different cities. I visit each one three to four times a year and stay at an AirBnb near them. I take my kids and their friends out to dinner each time, and I pick up the bill.*

Okay, now it's your turn. Write down below (or use a separate sheet if needed) a description of what your life will look like:

_____
_____
_____
_____
_____
_____
_____
_____
_____
_____
_____
_____
_____
_____
_____
_____
_____
_____
_____
_____
_____

_____

_____

_____

_____

_____

_____

_____

_____

_____

_____

_____

_____

_____

_____

_____

_____

Okay, now we are going to take your vision of the future, and we are going to calculate how much money you need to actually live this life. Most people never do this. And most people think they need ten million dollars to live a life of financial independence. This isn't the case.

Think through what you wrote above, and let's start putting some numbers to it.

Create your monthly budget below:

Category	How much you'll spend	Example
Grocery shopping		$1,000
Eating out		$500
Entertainment (movies, etc.)		$200
Gyms + personal fitness		$200
Gas		$120
Clothes		$150
Utilities (heating, A/C, etc.)		$300
Cell phone		$100
Hobbies		$150
Mortgage		$0 (house paid off)
Car payment		$0 (cars bought used and paid with cash)
Property Taxes		$200
Insurance (car/home)		$200
HOA		$0
Health Insurance		$700
Other categories:		
Monthly Total (add them all up)		$3,820

Now, once you have your monthly total, do the following steps:

Yearly Fixed Expenses = Monthly Total x 12

So, in the example above, the Yearly Fixed Expenses would be $45,840 (= $3,820 x 12).

Write down your Yearly Fixed Expenses below:

Yearly Fixed Expenses = _____

Next, we are going to factor in other discretionary things. So, in this hypothetical example, it was important to the person to travel eight weeks a year and visit their kids at college. Our hypothetical person would budget an additional $25,000 a year to do this traveling.

Write down below your Yearly Discretionary Spending.

Yearly Discretionary Spending = _____

Next, we add them all together to get your Yearly Spending goal.

Yearly Spending = Yearly Fixed Expenses + Yearly Discretionary Spending

So in this example it would look like:

Yearly Spending − $45,840 + $25,000 = $70,840

Write down your number below:

Yearly Spending = _____

Okay, here's the important part. We are going to translate your yearly spending into how much money you need to have saved and invested to be able to support this spending.

This is your Freedom Number.

How do we do this? Well, we rely on the famous Trinity Study[1] that showed that people could withdraw 4% of their investment portfolio each year and not run the risk of outliving their savings. This 4% allows us to relate our spending to our investment funds and back and forth.

How? Well, it's simple. Suppose we want to spend $70,840/year. We can use the results from the Trinity Study to now reverse engineer how much our investment portfolio needs to be worth for us to be able to spend $70,840/year. We do this by asking the question "How much does my portfolio need to be worth if 4% of my portfolio is $70,840? It turns out this is just a simple math problem we all learned how to solve in elementary school.

Another way to think about the 4% is that you need *25 times* your annual spending saved.

Hence in this example:

---

[1] Cooley, Philip L., Carl M. Hubbard, and Daniel T. Walz. 'Retirement Savings: Choosing a Withdrawal Rate That Is Sustainable.' AAII Journal, February 1998.

Freedom Number = $70,840 x 25 = $1,771,000

So, in this example, to be able to afford to spend $70,840/year and not run out of money we need to have saved $1,771,000. Now, this may seem like a lot, but due to compounding interest you won't need to save anywhere close to that (I'll show you how).

Now it is your time to calculate your Freedom Number.

My Freedom Number = Yearly Spending x 25 = _____

Congratulations! By sitting down and doing this simple calculation you've accomplished something great:

1. You've written an intentional spending statement that aligns with what you want your habits, roles, and routines to look like.

2. Most people don't get to where they are going because they haven't defined where they want to go. Your Freedom Number tells you what your goal is. 99% of people never take the time to get this type of clarity.

3. If you are like most, you are probably shocked at your Freedom Number. You may be thinking: *Oh geez, there's no way I can save that amount of money.* But here's the thing. You don't have to save that entire amount. Due to investing and compound interest, you will actually only need to save a portion of that amount and let time and compound interest do the rest.

How To Reach Your Freedom Number: The Magic of Compound Interest

Okay, the first step in your journey toward becoming a wealthy OT is determining where you are going. That's your Freedom Number.

The next step is determining how the hell you get there. It all comes down to the three pillars: earning more, saving more, and investing more as an OT. And that's what the rest of this book is about.

After understanding your Freedom Number, the next most important thing to understand is the magic of compound interest. Compound interest is how you multiply your money over time. Compound interest has been described by Einstein as "the eighth wonder of the world."

Compounding happens when your money earns returns, and those returns are reinvested to earn even more. Over time, this cycle of growth accelerates, allowing your investments to grow faster the longer they stay invested. Let me give you a quick example. Let's say you invest $1,000 and it earns a return of 10% a year. Well, at the end of the first year you will have $1,100. That's great—you've earned $100 the first year.

But, if you keep the entire $1,100 invested then at the end of year two, you will have $1,210. Between years one and two, you increased your earnings by $110—more than the $100 you earned in the first year. And that's because the gains you earned in year one are now compounding in year two.

The great thing about this is: the longer you stay invested, the greater the impact. Let's say you keep that same $1,000 invested for 20 years. Well, at the end of 20 years, that $1000 will have turned into $6,727. At year 19 you will have had $6116. That means that from year 19 to 20, you will have earned $611, not the original $100 each year you were earning. This is the magic of compounding.

Compound interest has been compared to building a snowball by legendary investor Warren Buffett. To build a big snowball you find a steep hill and let a small ball roll down. By the time it gets to the bottom, the snowball will have become huge compared to what you started with at the top. This is what compound interest does to your money.

In fact, going back to Einstein, his full quote is: "Compound interest is the eighth wonder of the world. He who understands it, earns it. . . he who doesn't. . . pays it." In other words, you definitely want to understand it.

People mistakenly think that if they want to retire with a million dollars then they literally either have to have earned a million dollars or saved a million dollars. And that's just wrong!

Let me give you an example. Would you rather have:

1. $1,000,000 today, or

2. the value of a penny doubling every day for 30 days?

Most people instinctively select the first option, a million dollars today. It's easy to think that a penny doubling every day for 30 days will amount to, well, pennies—or at most a few dollars.

Here's the kicker: a penny that doubles every day for 30 days will be worth $5.4 million in 30 days! This is what compound interest does and why it is so powerful!

Here is the table which shows what a penny does doubling each day:

Day	Value
1	$0.01
2	$0.02
3	$0.04
4	$0.08
5	$0.16
6	$0.32
7	$0.64
8	$1.28

Day	Value
9	$2.56
10	$5.12
11	$10.24
12	$20.48
13	$40.96
14	$81.92
15	$163.84
16	$327.68
17	$655.36
18	$1,310.72
19	$2,621.44
20	$5,242.88
21	$10,485.76
22	$20,971.52
23	$41,943.04
24	$83,886.08
25	$167,772.16
26	$335,544.32
27	$671,088.64

Day	Value
28	$1,342,177.28
29	$2,684,354.56
30	$5,368,709.12

This table highlights a few interesting things:

1. Growth is slow in the beginning. It isn't until day 21 (two-thirds of the way to 30 days) that we even break $10k.
2. Growth, given time, reaches a breaking point where gains take off. It takes 27 days to reach $671k, but only 3 days to reach $5.4 million.

This is HUGE and here are the major takeaways for OTs:

1. Small savings today can have a huge impact in the future and on your future—but it will take a while, likely years, before you see their impact.
2. You have to keep the faith, and this is why automating your savings and investing is so critical to keep you on track.
3. Your time horizon matters. If you had stopped after 10 days, you would have a tiny fraction of what you would have after 30 days. Start NOW and think decades ahead.

Alright, let's recap what we've covered so far:

We started by redefining wealth for OTs, focusing on the freedom and flexibility wealth provides rather than on material possessions. We, then, walked through the critical exercise of calculating your Freedom Number—the amount you need to have saved and invested to live life on your own terms.

Finally, we explored the magic of compound interest and how it can transform your savings over time. Remember, small savings today can have a huge impact down the road, but you need to give it time to work its magic.

Start now, stay the course, and keep the faith. In the coming chapters, we'll dive into the nitty-gritty of how to earn more, save more, and invest more as an OT. Get ready to take control of your financial future and attain financial freedom!

CHAPTER ONE

THE BIG SQUEEZE FOR OTs AND WHY MONEY IS AN ESSENTIAL ADL[2]

> *"You must gain control over your money, or the lack of it will forever control you."*
>
> \- Dave Ramsey

This I know for certain: you didn't go to OT school to become rich.

If money were a primary motivating factor for you, there's a whole host of other healthcare professions through which you could still make a positive impact while earning a higher salary. You could have become a surgeon, a psychiatrist, a dentist, a certified nurse anesthetist, or even a pharmacist.

---

2 While money itself is not technically an "activity", I'm taking a bit of literary license here to be thought-provoking. Managing, earning, saving, and investing money are all activities that impact daily living, much like traditional ADLs. Rather than listing each individually, I've chosen to use 'money' as a catch-all term to keep things clear and concise.

Every single OT I speak to tells me some variation of:

- I felt called to be an OT
- I want to look at the entire person, not a narrow aspect of their life/health
- I felt OT was the most creative of all healthcare specialties, with the most diverse work settings
- I choose OT for workplace flexibility

As an OT, I bet you are good at putting the needs of other people first. You may struggle, though, with setting boundaries and feeling guilty about prioritizing your needs. And guilt plays a huge role in how we think about money. In fact, most OTs I speak with would rather make an impact than be wealthy.

I'm here to show you that you can do both. And in fact, building wealth as an OT will allow you to make an even greater impact.

Money is an Essential ADL

As an OT, suppose a client came to you with these challenges:

- They're unable to maintain a healthy diet due to the cost of nutritious food, relying instead on cheaper, less wholesome options

- They're anxious about the rising costs of their necessary prescription medications, which they sometimes skip due to budget constraints
- The idea of an unplanned house repair, like a leaking roof or broken heating system, fills them with dread
- They long to visit their grandchildren who live a few states away, but the travel costs make it an impossible dream

The challenges, while unique, all share an "invisible" activity of daily living that too often isn't discussed. And that ADL is Money.

Maslow's Hierarchy of Needs: The Hidden Role of Money

Money allows us to buy nutritious food. It enables us to afford healthcare necessities, providing safety and security. Money fuels opportunities for social engagement, such as visiting loved ones or attending community activities, fulfilling the need for love and belonging. It gives us the means to engage in personal interests, catering to esteem needs. Lastly, it provides the freedom and stability to realize one's potential beyond survival, paving the way for self-actualization.

In fact, if you look at Maslow's Hierarchy of Needs, I would challenge you to find one that doesn't require money.

Despite money being as vital as the oxygen we breathe, many OTs feel guilty thinking about money. It isn't your fault that you may feel guilty thinking about it. Most of us have limiting beliefs when it comes to money, which we will explore in Chapter 2. For now, know that once these limiting beliefs and prior money traumas are dealt with, a huge liberation occurs in your ability to build wealth as an OT.

The Vicious Cycle of High Debt + Low Salary

If our limiting money beliefs are the internal barrier to building wealth, then we must discuss the elephant in the room for the biggest external factor. In fact, there are two big barriers that you must overcome on your path to financial freedom.

The Twin Titans Threatening Your Financial Future

The biggest external barrier to OTs building wealth is the vice-like grip of two compounding factors:

- High debt (student loans + others) that consumes a large amount of your monthly salary
- Low salaries, especially relative to debt levels, that tend to stay stagnant rather than increase over time

Make no mistake—this is a dangerous mix. And both of these should be treated like the emergency they are.

It is common for a new OT grad (especially coming from an OTD program) to graduate with over $100k of student loan debt. If you have $125k of student loans with 7% interest and a 20-year repayment period, you would be paying approximately $969/month. The total amount of interest you'd pay over those twenty years would be $105k—almost equal to the cost of your degree!

If you, instead, repay this over a 10-year period, you would have a monthly payment of $1,451. You'd pay a total of an extra $49k in interest charges.

On top of this monthly payment, we have to add other expenses:

- Housing
- Car
- Maintenance and insurance
- Daycare (if needed)
- Food
- Utilities

And pretty soon, the monthly expenses start to get quite high.

The Harsh Reality of OT Compensation

Let's look at the other side of the equation—your income. Surely, the burden of hundreds of thousands of dollars in student loans must come with outsized salaries. Right?

Wrong.

According to the US Bureau of Labor Statistics, in 2022 there were over 130k OTs employed in the US with a median annual salary of $93,180.[3] The corresponding hourly wage was $44.80.

To achieve higher salaries, typically you would have to move to states with a much higher cost of living. For instance, in 2022, California was the highest paying state with an annual mean salary of $109k.

However, if you find yourself saying: "Whoo... I don't earn that type of money as an OT," then you aren't alone. This data doesn't differentiate by years of experience. According to a survey that the AOTA conducted in 2018, the median salary for a new OT grad was just $65,000 a year. This would increase, on average, by $8,000 after six years of working.

Indeed, most OTs I speak to report that they make anywhere from $37 to $42 per hour. And these OT jobs typically come with high productivity requirements, onerous documentation, and limited flexibility in terms of scheduling.

---

3   U.S. Bureau of Labor Statistics. (2022). Occupational employment and wage statistics: Occupational therapists (29-1122). Retrieved from https://www.bls.gov/oes/2022/may/oes291122.htm

This is because healthcare in the United States is a business. Not only is it a business, but it is a business that is controlled by insurance companies.

Insurance companies are the proverbial tail wagging the dog. Insurance companies determine the reimbursement rates for most OTs working in the United States today. They determine what is "covered" and what isn't.

And the insurance company's incentive is to reduce costs, and the way they do this is to continually reduce reimbursement and deny coverage.

This reliance on insurance has two negative effects for OTs:

- It encourages a healthcare model based on volume. This leads to increasingly high productivity requirements which increases burnout.
- It will ALWAYS put a cap on what an OT can earn. And this is because the amazing work you are doing for your client isn't paid for by the client, but rather by a third-party (the insurance company) who isn't receiving the care.

So is this story all doom and gloom? Is the fate of all OTs truly sealed?

Absolutely not. In fact, OTs are in an incredible position to build wealth. Despite these headwinds, as an OT you are still in one of the higher paid industries in the United States. And, as you'll see in Chapter 3, there are numerous other professions that are compensated less than OTs who are successful at building wealth. If they can do it, so can you!

You are in a unique position, and your plan to build wealth has to be focused on a combination of the following:

1. Increase your savings and investing rate (or begin if you have not yet). Your savings and investing rate is the most important component to building your wealth as an OT. I cover your savings in Chapter 5 and your investing in Chapters 4 and 8.

2. Immediately, and urgently, eliminate your debt to free up money each month to save and invest (this is covered in Chapter 6 and 7)

3. Increase your income as an OT. You have amazing skills and the transformation you provide to your clients is worth more than $40/hr. If a massage therapist can make $90/hour, then there is absolutely no reason you can't increase your income. Some ways include specialization, PRN, and private pay (see Chapter 9 to discover my favorite!).

I think you'll find more joy, more happiness, and more impact as an OT when you focus on building your wealth.

The Impact of Financial Stress on Professional Performance and Well-Being

As an OT, you are probably acutely aware of the things that can negatively impact a session with a client. If you didn't get a good sleep the night before, then those first few sessions are going to be difficult. If you fought with your spouse or kid before leaving for work, despite your best efforts, you'll carry some of that into your sessions. If your elderly parents have suddenly taken a turn for the worse, it may be difficult to concentrate during your motivational interviewing.

And this is, of course, completely natural; you are human. Despite all our best efforts, what is happening in our personal lives bleeds over to our professional lives. We may all have various abilities to minimize the impact, but pretending there isn't an impact is a lie that we can tell ourselves to pretend we are more superhuman than we are.

Likewise, your relationship with money is impacting your professional performance as an OT.

How Money Worries Sabotage Your OT Career

Financial stress is incredibly common. Consider the following statistics:

- 62% of Americans report losing sleep over financial stress—their retirement accounts, bills, credit cards, and healthcare costs.
- 48% of all employees report worrying about money.
- 73% of Americans report money as a significant source of stress, causing headaches, depression, and other health issues.
- Arguments about money are the largest predictor of divorce in married couples—more so than other marital disagreements.

The Silent Epidemic Affecting OTs Everywhere

From these statistics, it seems that just about everyone is stressed about money. Failing to put a sensible plan in place for your finances—and ability to sleep well at night knowing your financial future is secured—means you risk running into a chronic money stress problem.

And we know the impact that chronic stress has. Our sympathetic nervous system will stay in a state of constant activation of the stress response, and we won't have adequate recovery or relaxation periods. This is a disastrous way to live. The impact on your well-being is marked.

I am a firm believer in the concept of being anti-fragile—a term coined by author Nassim Nicholas Taleb, which refers to systems, individuals, or organizations that don't just withstand stress and challenges but actually grow stronger because of them. In my experience, we tend to improve as individuals when we are tested or when we intentionally put ourselves in challenging situations. These experiences push us beyond our comfort zones, fostering growth, resilience, and personal development in ways that comfort and ease never could.

For example, if we avoid public speaking because we are afraid, then we experience no personal growth. If we start to expose ourselves to the stress of public speaking in moderated, incremental doses, then not only does our nervous system start to adapt, but we have an opportunity to acquire essential public speaking skills that can propel our career, such as the ability to influence, to remain calm in stressful situations, to think on our feet, and to communicate more effectively.

Not all stressors are equal. You may only have to do a public speaking event once per month, while money stress is pervasive. It envelopes you like air. It is all around you. Extreme stress can push you past a breaking point where the stress is no longer beneficial.

This is commonly true with stress related to money. If you end up in a chronic state of money stress, you'll find:

- Your cognitive function is impacted by an extended exposure to cortisol, which damages your hippocampus

- You experience burnout with OT for a variety of reasons, such as feeling stuck in a toxic work environment with unrealistic productivity requirements
- You experience physical symptoms such as digestive problems, trouble sleeping, and a weakened immune system, along with other potential health problems such as heart disease
- You may feel depressed or anxious and experience mood swings

Of course, there are small things you can do to reduce your stress, like engaging in hobbies, exercising, prioritizing your fitness and nutrition, and focusing on developing meaningful relationships.

These things are great, and you should do them. But these are Band-Aids that won't be sustainable if you don't address a more fundamental problem.

Escaping the Financial Trap: Your Path to Abundance

Imagine this. How much financial stress would you have if your student loans were fully paid off and every single month you were investing in your retirement and saving for your kids' college?

How much financial stress would you have if you had one year of living expenses saved so that you could change jobs without worry? Say goodbye to feeling stuck under a Director of Rehab that is a tyrant.

How much financial stress would you have if your cars were paid off and you had an emergency car repair fund?

How much financial stress would you have if your life was set up such that you paid cash for every single purchase, you were debt-free and every single month you had so much money left over that you saved $4k/month and still went on three vacations a year?

How much financial stress would you have if you could afford to drop down to three days a week when you have a child and still earn more in three days than when you were working five days?

How much financial stress would you have if instead of *having* to work, you were in a position to *choose* to work? Even dream jobs become a nightmare when you have no control over when or how you work.

These scenarios are possible, but only with a plan and some sacrifice. Too often we accept our situation as fixed and focus on ways to tolerate it. We get by. We survive rather than thrive.

I don't want you to tolerate your financial situation. I want you to improve it. I want you to live in abundance. I want you to have full control and autonomy over your future.

We've covered a lot of ground in this first chapter, and I know some of it might feel a bit heavy. Here's the deal—we've got to face these financial challenges head-on if we want to create a better future for ourselves and our profession. We've seen how money is woven into every aspect of our lives and how the crushing combination of high debt and low salaries can leave us feeling trapped and stressed out.

The good news is that you're not alone, and there is a way out. If we understand the root causes of our financial struggles and their impact on our lives, we can start to take control and make some real changes. In the coming chapters, we're going to dive into some practical strategies to help you pay off your debt, boost your income, and start investing in your future. It's not going to be easy, but it's going to be worth it.

Take a deep breath, grab a cup of coffee (or a glass of wine, if that's more your style), and let's keep going. Together, we're going to transform the way OTs think about money and create a new generation of financially independent OTs. And the first step to tackling this tough topic is doing some deep inner work.

CHAPTER TWO

OVERCOMING FINANCIAL TRAUMA: INNER WORK FOR OTs

"We don't see things as they are, we see them as we are."

– Anaïs Nin

There is a famous personal finance personality named Dave Ramsay who has coined the term "personal finance is 80% behavior and only 20% head knowledge." As someone who has achieved financial freedom, I fully agree with this. The math behind becoming financially independent is incredibly simple. There are only about six things you need to know, and you could write them down on an index card. How you behave is much more important than what you know when it comes to personal finance. This is true.

However, I've recently come to realize that the saying "personal finance is 80% behavior and only 20% head knowledge" looks great on a billboard but doesn't tell the entire story. And that's because the statement implies that we are essentially robots, and if we changed our behavior like we change a light bulb, then we'd suddenly be on the path to financial freedom.

You and I both know that it isn't this simple. Our behavior is greatly influenced by our thoughts and feelings. If we don't address these, then there is no hope to change our behavior in a lasting way. We would be in a constant fight with ourselves.

Another thing to keep in mind is that the thoughts and feelings we have around money were most likely developed when we were kids. These thoughts about money are invisible money stories we tell ourselves of which we're often not even aware. If you are aware of these money stories, you likely take them as objective, universal truth, instead of just your experience and something that can be changed.

Examining Your Money Trauma

As an OT, you are likely aware and sensitive to the role that trauma plays with your clients. Having a trauma-informed approach is essential to your plan of care.

I would gently and politely ask you to consider the following question: "Have you considered the impact of money trauma in your life?"

Most of us have experienced some type of money trauma when we were kids. Often, this is unresolved, unprocessed, and hanging out in the background. From this unresolved trauma we form certain money scripts to fit into our version of the world. This is so pervasive that once you see it, you won't be able to unsee it.

Let me give you some examples.

1. Katherine grew up in a house with a single mother. Money was always tight and her mom was often having to work two jobs to afford to put food on the table. Katherine wasn't able to play soccer growing up because her mom couldn't afford the registration fees and uniform. When Katherine started to work, she became extremely frugal and denied herself any form of luxury due to fears of going back to the poverty level.

2. Sam grew up in a house with a single mother. Like Katherine, there was no money left after basic necessities. When Sam started working and had kids, Sam took the opposite approach and showered his kids with the gifts and opportunities he didn't have growing up. He stretched beyond his financial capability to live in the "right" neighborhood and provide the childhood he didn't have, and as a result he lived in constant debt.

3. Ruth grew up with two parents who always struggled to make ends meet. One car would often be in need of repairs that they couldn't afford. The utilities in the house were often shut off because their bill was overdue. Ruth started to associate money with stress, unreliability, and conflict. As she grew up, she unconsciously avoided

situations to earn more because money made her anxious and uncomfortable.

4. David's parents divorced when he was ten. His dad traveled a lot for work so David spent most of his time living with his mom. When his dad would come to visit, they would often get into disagreements about why David's dad couldn't come to more school functions. David's dad felt jealous of the relationship that David had with his mom and would often lash out at David. To make up, David's dad would then buy him expensive presents to make up. David grew up feeling that money and material possessions were used for power and manipulation.

5. Jenny grew up in a middle class neighborhood. In high school she fell into the popular crowd, and her peers all had the latest clothes and gadgets. Jenny felt like she needed to fit in and would pressure her parents to buy her cool items that they couldn't easily afford. Over time, she drifted away from the popular crowd. As Jenny started to work, though, she developed a habit of overspending to maintain a certain social image and feel accepted by her peers.

We all have our own unique experience. If you are like most people, you probably haven't taken the time to examine your earliest memories related to money and the associated emotions.

If you want to be in balance with money, view it objectively, and finally be able to build wealth, then it is critical you turn the spotlight inward and consider your history.

Here is a quick exercise you can do:

1. Find a quiet place where you feel safe and secure;
2. Close your eyes;
3. Start to replay some of your earliest and strongest negative memories in your mind;
4. Visualize them as if you are back there;
5. As you are visualizing, ask yourself a few prompting questions:
   - What role is money playing in this memory?
   - What were your feelings toward money during this time in your life?
   - Does this memory involve a significant purchase? Why and what emotions are associated with this memory?
   - Did a lack or abundance of money affect the outcome of this memory? How and why?
   - Did you feel like you were empowered or disempowered in this memory? How did money play a role?
6. Write down your observations and insights from this exercise.

This exercise is incredibly powerful and can be emotional. Give yourself grace if you find it too difficult. Come back to it at a later point.

OTs who have gone through this exercise have described incredible insights:

- "I realize that I haven't been willing to ask for a raise because my dad was laid off when I was eight, which was stressful. Those memories make me feel just happy to have a job."
- "My mom had a shopping problem and would hide her purchases from my dad, which always caused big fights. I haven't wanted to look at my bank account each month because I'm scared of what I might find."
- "My dad was in sales and sometimes he'd earn a big commission and buy things that were too expensive that we'd have to return later. I want to show him that I'm more responsible, which is why I buy things I can't actually afford and then work overtime so I can pay for them."

The Under-Earners, Under-Savers, and Under-Accumulators

Most OTs I speak with fall into one of these camps:

- An under-earner of money
- An under-saver of money
- An under-accumulator of money

If society tells us that overly focusing on money is bad, then the opposite, being an under-accumulator of money must be good, right?

Not quite.

The overtly greedy person and the person who under-accumulates wealth represent two sides of the same coin: they are both out of balance with money. They see money as either the answer to their problems or the root of all problems. Like with almost everything, the answer is somewhere in the middle.

For OTs who are under-earners, under-savers, and under-accumulators of wealth, the reality is that this is usually avoidance behavior due to money trauma. You may be consciously or unconsciously avoiding thoughts, situations, and experiences that require you to face your past money traumas. Instead of developing a healthy, balanced attitude toward money and wealth, it's common to stay stuck in old thought patterns that don't serve you anymore.

A healthy relationship with money and wealth accumulation involves realizing that it is a tool like any other. Want to do good in this world and make a positive impact? Great—you can do that with money. Want to be selfish and greedy? You could do that with money, too. The commonality here is what YOU decide to use it for. Money on its own doesn't do anything. It is just an extension, an instrument, of yourself.

Money: A Tool for Magnifying Your Impact

Want to make a greater impact in the world? Great—arm yourself with more money, and you'll have more resources to create change and make a positive difference. Money is a lever. It magnifies and provides leverage to what you want to accomplish. Feeling altruistic and want to travel to Haiti and build clean water drinking wells? That's great, but as an individual, there is a limit to your impact. However, if you've saved $150k, then suddenly you can afford to hire help. Instead of one person building wells, you could have five hundred people building wells simultaneously. You have the same goal with bigger impact because you have greater leverage (e.g. money) to accomplish your goals.

Money doesn't have feelings. Money doesn't have an agenda. Money doesn't have a political bent. Money doesn't have a bias. It is people who have feelings, an agenda and a political bent. Becoming aware of this distinction is one of the first steps to overcoming the limiting belief that money is evil and, instead, using your money for more impact.

Examining Limiting Money Beliefs

I could give you all the strategies in the world to become a wealthy OT, but if you don't think it is achievable for yourself, you'll never try.

This is where limiting beliefs come in. Limiting money beliefs are the thoughts you have around money that currently limit your full potential to achieve wealth as an OT. Often, you might not even be aware that you have these limiting beliefs. And, if you are aware of these thoughts, then it is easy to feel that your thoughts about money are absolute and fixed, rather than based on your unique experience and, indeed, changeable.

Limiting beliefs get instilled in us early: from our own childhood experiences with money (e.g. money trauma), from our family members passing down their feelings about money, and from the media we consume. If you are going to embark on building wealth as an OT, though, then we need to tackle these limiting beliefs head on.

Limiting Belief #1: I do good for the world, so I don't need to focus on money

This one is quite pervasive in caring professions such as OT. There can be guilt associated with thinking about money.

And often, those in OT feel so called to be an OT that it feels, well, a little dirty to think about money or focus on your financial future. After all, isn't doing good for their world enough?

Sadly, the answer is no. Focusing on building wealth as an OT doesn't make you greedy. I'll show you in later chapters that the primary way to become wealthy is using your existing OT income. Nothing greedy about that—it is being resourceful with your existing resources.

In fact, I think building wealth as an OT is one of the most personally responsible things you can do. Building wealth as an OT allows you to:

- Have flexibility and autonomy to pick the work situations where you shine the most as a professional
- Withstand financial emergencies such as unexpected car repairs, a new roof on your house, or braces for your kids without adding stress to your life
- Be able to go on adventures with your kids. Life is meant to be filled with joy and adventure, and there is absolutely nothing wrong with working hard, being rewarded for it, and playing hard.
- Spend more time with your family. As a dad, I'm acutely aware that the vast majority of the time I spend with my kids will happen before they turn 18. Building wealth allows you to spend more quality time with your kids by having the financial ability to drop down part-time, take summers off, etc.

- Obtain the best care for yourself without being a burden to those around you. Here's the sad fact: we all age, which you see firsthand as an OT. And when we age we need more and more care.

You can do good in the world and build wealth as an OT. The two aren't mutually exclusive.

Limiting Belief #2: Money is the Root of All Evil

If you turn on the news, open a newspaper, or watch just about any movie with a bad guy in it, you'll find numerous examples of people driven by greed rather than by ethics.

It is no surprise that we come to associate money as being "evil." We carry this around subconsciously, and it makes us unwilling to focus on money. We keep our distance. After all, why would you want to get close to something associated with greed?

Money is like a chef's knife. In the right hands, a chef's knife can be used to create an amazing meal that not only fuels your nutrition but brings together a community (think of a neighborhood block party). A skilled chef can turn simple ingredients into a feast, just as someone can use money to turn a simple idea into a thriving business or help a struggling community thrive. On the other hand, in the wrong hands, the chef's knife can cause irreparable harm, just like money can cause damage when used unethically. It isn't the knife that's good or bad—it's how it's used, and by whom, that makes all the difference.

I would politely challenge you to view money as a tool with which you can do good. Here is a major downside to sticking with this limiting belief that money is the root of all evil: many people avoid learning about personal finance, savings, taxes, etc. due to fear that they are participating or perpetuating an evil system. This approach furthers your own financial instability and stress, which will further reinforce your negative view of money.

Limiting Belief #3: I Don't Make Enough to Become Wealthy

Too many people think that building wealth and becoming financially independent is beyond their reach, so they don't even start. This is especially true for OTs. You may think you need to be a CEO, an entertainer, or someone famous to have any hope of financial independence.

This couldn't be further from the truth. The number 1 wealth building tool at your disposal is your OT salary. Building wealth is less about the total amount you make and more about how much you save and invest.

Someone who makes $400,000 a year but spends $399,000 every year will never become wealthy. But the OT who makes $85,000 a year and saves and invests $15,000 each year will become wealthy in the long run.

Building wealth requires discipline and sticking to your plans in the long run. It isn't overnight.

Limiting Belief #4: I'm Not Good with Money

You've gone through graduate school to get your OT degree. You've taken numerous continuing education courses to refine your skills. You have the ability to walk into new client situations, ask the right questions, build connections and rapport with your clients, and develop innovative and creative treatment plans that fit into your client's lives.

I've got a good news secret: that is all more complicated than being good with money. The close cousin of this limiting belief is the belief that being smart with money is complicated.

Often, when someone tells me that they "aren't good with money," what is happening under the surface is a combination of two things:

- There is some past money trauma holding them back from looking at their financial situation with clear eyes.
- They are living out of alignment with their values. Their spending doesn't actually reflect their priorities, and they don't know where to start.

The truth is that being smart with money relies on three things. They are all easy to understand and grasp. You don't need to be an accountant, a tax advisor, or some math wizard.

It comes down to:

1. Living on less than you earn
2. Saving and investing a certain percentage of your income in diversified, low-fee investments
3. Repeating the above for many years

Becoming good with money is a skill you can learn. And you are already light years ahead of others by reading this book.

Limiting Belief #5: I will Prioritize This in the Future. I Have Time!

It is seductive to think that you have time to start prioritizing your financial future. You may find yourself thinking some combination of the following:

- I just graduated. I'm going to treat myself and when I get to a certain income I will start saving. I've got decades to figure this out.
- I've got kids and lots of expenses. When they are older and things settle down, I'll start saving. It is too tight right now.
- There's always great demand for OTs, so if things get tight, I will pick up some extra work. I'll figure out the finances in the future.

Here's the thing: time is not on your side. The cost of procrastination is huge.

The key to building long-term, sustainable wealth as an OT is to invest over many years. And the later you start, the less your money will grow.

It doesn't matter if you are 25 or 55—start savings and investing today. Don't delay.

To bring this home, let me give you a comparison:

- Sarah is 25 years old and saves $10,000 a year from age 25 to 45, at which time she stops adding contributions. With an average return of 10% her portfolio will grow to $2.2 million by the time she is 60.
- Lisa gets a later start and doesn't start investing until she is 40 years old. From age 40 to age 60, she saves $20,000 a year—double what Sarah was doing. Despite this, at age 60, Lisa's portfolio will only be worth $1.1 million.

Despite Lisa investing double what Sarah invested, Lisa still ends up with 50% of Sarah's portfolio.

Why?

This is because Sarah was invested in the market for much longer. Sarah was invested in the market for 35 years compared to 20 years for Lisa.

Despite Sarah contributing less each year, she comes out ahead because she was invested longer.

So, no matter if you are 25, 35, or 55, start right now. If you've been waiting to start then make the commitment that that time is today. Don't focus on time you may have lost. That's in the past.

Armed with this knowledge, take the most advantage of maximizing the amount of time you have by starting *today*.

Limiting Belief #6: Investing is Risky and Like Gambling

We've had multiple financial crashes in the last 25 years. We had the dot-com bust in the early 2000s, followed by the large financial market crash in 2008 and then fears of a recession due to the COVID-19 pandemic starting in 2020.

Even without these crashes, many people are uncomfortable with risk and feel the best thing to do is keep their money under their proverbial mattress.

In fact, there is a term for this: "loss aversion." The psychologists Daniel Kahneman and Amos Tversky discovered that the pain people feel from losing something is twice as great as the pleasure they receive from gaining something.

This is amazing. Let's think about it. We feel twice as much pain from losing $100 than we do the pleasure in getting $100. This keeps many people on the fence and reluctant to invest. *What if I lose money? What if things don't work out? What if the value never recovers?*

This fear of losing can be enough to prevent you from opening your first 401(k) account or buying some investments in your IRA.

However, not all risk is the same.

1. Putting all your money in an individual stock—that is equivalent to going to the casino in Las Vegas and putting your money on black.
2. Putting your money in broad index funds that replicate the US economy? That is different. You still have risk, of course, but you aren't relying on the performance of any individual company's stock, which reduces your risk.
3. The risk of not investing: this is HUGE. Those who sit out on the sidelines and reframe from investing *always* lose in the long-term. This is because inflation will eat away at your purchasing ability. Historically inflation averages about 3% per year (1914 – 2023). The $25,000 car today? In 10 years it will cost roughly $33,958! If you aren't investing your money today, then your money in the future will simply be worth less. And that leads to a poorer quality of life in the future.

As we will talk about in later chapters, there are smart ways to diversify and reduce your risk.

We've looked at how our past experiences with money shape our current beliefs and behaviors, often in ways we're not even aware of. We've examined the limiting beliefs that hold us back from achieving financial freedom and building wealth as OTs.

Here's the thing: these beliefs are just that—beliefs. They're not set in stone, and they don't define your future.

You have the power to rewrite your money story, confront your limiting beliefs head-on, and start taking action toward your financial goals. It won't always be easy, and it won't happen overnight, but with consistency and dedication, you can become an OT with financial freedom.

Remember, building wealth isn't about being greedy or neglecting your calling as an OT. In fact, it's quite the opposite. By taking control of your finances, you're putting yourself in a position to do even more good in the world and have a greater impact on the lives of your clients and your community.

Next, we are going to dispel even more myths about what it takes to become financially free, given all the noise that's out there. I think you'll be surprised.

Let's do this!

CHAPTER THREE

SECRETS TO WEALTH ACCUMULATION: TAILORED ADVICE FOR OTs

"Wealth is not about having a lot of money; it's about having a lot of options."

– Chris Rock

Forget Everything You Think You Know About Becoming Wealthy

I want you to forget everything you think you know about becoming wealthy. That's because, often, our thoughts about becoming wealthy are influenced by some pretty unreliable data points:

- The conversation with your uncle at the Thanksgiving table who tells you to "marry a doctor"
- The media that constantly oscillates between showing you corrupt rich people and a TV host talking about a single stock and how it is posed to increase 300%

- The one "rich" person you know who drives a fancy car and lives in a gated community
- Our family members who tell us to use credit cards so we can "go on vacation using points" or that timeshares are good investments
- Social media posts touting "37 different passive income streams you can do in your pajamas while eating Ben and Jerry's"

You have to be wary of a lot of advice out there. That's because they are often either (a) trying to sell you something and are hiding it under "information" or (b) giving you advice that would be hard to replicate.

Instead, focus on what you can learn from the "normal" people who have become wealthy in their lifetime. What timeless principles are in play here and how can we apply those to our life?

The perception of wealthy people is at odds with the reality of wealthy people. Often, it is easy to focus on the exceptions (athletes, tech founders, CEOs, etc.) rather than the rule. If you want to become a wealthy OT, then focusing on the rules of building wealth is key.

In the book *Millionaire Next Door: The Surprising Secrets of America's Wealthy*, the authors pulled back the veil surrounding how wealthy people actually live. First published in 1996, it challenged people's preconceived notions that millionaires are born, rather than self-made.

More recently, in 2018, Ramsay Solutions conducted the largest study of millionaires ever. They interviewed over ten thousand millionaires to shine a light on their careers, how they became wealthy, what they do with their money and how they live.

Shattering the Millionaire Myth: Surprising Facts About the Wealthy

Here are some surprising facts about millionaires taken from these two studies.

1. Only 31% earned more than $100,000 annually in their careers on average

The average millionaire isn't a high earning professional. Of course, you'll find high earners in the mix of millionaires. That isn't the norm, though. The norm is people making a middle-class to upper-middle-class living who prioritize building wealth over the long-run. In fact, the top five most common careers of millionaires includes teachers, who we know consistently don't make high salaries.

2. 75% attributed their millionaire status to regular and consistent investing over the long term

The millionaires portrayed are neither lottery winners nor those who sold an app and became wealthy overnight. Those are the exceptions, not the norm.

In fact, becoming a millionaire is a decades-long endeavor. It requires discipline and staying the course over the long run. The good news is that if you do, you'll join this group.

3. 75% have never carried credit card debt

Credit cards are a modern-day trap. They woo you with all these benefits and exclusive-sounding names. "Platinum," anyone? They encourage you to live well beyond your means. And it is the banks and credit card companies who reap the rewards. Remember, no one ever became wealthy on credit card points.

4. 94% live on less than they make. 93% use coupons each time they shop. And they spend under $200 each month eating out.

The Invisible Wealth: It's What You Don't Spend That Counts

In our culture we confuse spending with wealth. If we see someone wearing a custom suit we think: *Wow, they must have a lot of money to afford that.* The reality is that they *spent* that money. They no longer have it. Instead, they have a consumable item that loses its value.

Instead of spending, the wealthy focus on saving and investing. In that way, wealth is actually what you *don't* see. Wealth is the spending you don't see. A lot of the people you see driving nice cars and living in fancy houses aren't wealthy: they are stuck in a cycle of living paycheck to paycheck because they have nothing left at the end of each month.

In contrast, the wealthy set a savings and investing rate first. They prioritize "paying themselves first" by setting aside a certain percentage of their income each month to invest for their future. They know the greatest reward money can give them is their time in the future—not the immediate gratification gained from spending on items today.

The key to becoming wealthy is to be boring with your money:

- Live on less than you make.
- Save and invest regularly.
- Prioritize your spending on what is meaningful to you.

Stop Consuming and Start Owning

Compared to 150 years ago, we live in an amazing abundance that is easily underappreciated.

In the 1870s, it would take six months to travel from NYC to California in a covered wagon. Today you can make the same journey in six hours on a plane.

In the 1870s, many people died of malnutrition or foodborne diseases due to lack of preservation. Today, you are more likely to die due to an abundance of food that is largely unhealthy and causes heart disease, obesity, and diabetes at alarming rates.

In the 1870s, only 2% of 17-year-olds graduated from high school. Today it is closer to 85%. Likewise, in the 1870s most information was limited to books and the newspaper, which were expensive and limited. Today, everyone has the entire knowledge of their world in the palm of their hands through smart phones.

I always think of the following three words to realize how easy we have it now compared to the past: "surgery without anesthesia." Our lives are constantly improving. Technology is becoming better. We are becoming more efficient. Products are getting better. Our quality of life is constantly improving.

This is reflected in the stock market. All those innovations are, of course, being done by people. Guess what? Those people work at companies. And when those companies produce something meaningful, then the value of the company goes up.

Take Apple, for instance. In the early 2000s, Apple was a little bit of a black sheep in Silicon Valley. They were considered niche players with products like the Mac computer and the iPod. In 2002 its market capitalization was only $6 billion—reflecting that they hadn't knocked anything out of the park.

In July 2007, Apple made history and released the first iPhone. And it sold like hotcakes. By the end of 2007, the market capitalization of Apple increased to a whopping $75 billion. At the time of this writing, Apple's market capitalization is $2.91 trillion!

And guess what? This increase in value comes from one simple thing: it is a reflection of how much money people like you and me give to Apple for their products. That is, how many Apple products we consume. If Apple keeps making products that people want to buy, then it will keep being successful.

But where did this $2.91 trillion in capitalization go? Where is that money? The answer is that it went to the owners of Apple. And the owners are simply those investors in Apple who have purchased shares in Apple in the stock market.

So, let's consider this scenario: what if, instead of buying the iPhone in 2007, you bought shares in Apple?

Well, the iPhone retailed for $499 in 2007. If you took that same money and bought shares in Apple then those shares would be worth $5,152 today! Ask yourself, would you rather have turned $499 into $5,152 over a 16-year period, or have a good-looking paper weight?

And this example gets even better, because there are people who are buying new iPhones every single time a new version is released. If you'd bought five or six new phones over the years, this could easily amount to about $25,000 in lost investments!

Now, I'm not suggesting that you forego all new purchases. I'm not expecting you to live like a monk. I am saying, though, that a life of consumption will make *others* wealthy. A life of becoming an owner in companies you already like will lead to *you* becoming wealthy.

Ask yourself this: if you love their product so much, why not also own a piece of the company? Employees get paychecks; owners get a piece of the company. And *you want* a piece of the company. This is available to anyone with a few dollars and an internet connection. It has never been easier to invest.

Redefining Retirement: It's a Number, Not an Age

This may come as a surprise, but the idea of retirement is relatively new.

For much of history, people have worked until they died. Of course, life expectancy was much shorter back then, but the idea that you'd "move to Florida, play bingo, and have happy hour each day at 4 p.m." would've been absurd.

With economic progress come first world problems. People don't want to work until they die. They want to have time to pursue their hobbies. They want time to do the travel they've been putting off while raising kids and growing a career.

When Social Security was developed in 1935, the age 65 was introduced not because the government wanted folks to move to Florida, but due to more pressing concerns: rampant unemployment among younger workers and a desire to open up jobs for them by getting older people to leave their jobs. And so this age, 65, has become embedded in our minds that that is when you "retire."

This is incorrect. Retirement is a number, not an age. You can retire at age 50 if you have the means to support yourself without working. How? By safely withdrawing money from your portfolio of investments.

Remember the famous Trinity Study mentioned in Chapter 1? This study explored the impact of varying rates of withdrawal on a retirement portfolio. The purpose of the study was to recommend a "safe" withdrawal rate such that it wasn't likely you would outlive your money. And the study found that you could withdraw 4% of your retirement savings each year.

So, how does this exactly work in practice? It gives you a formula to convert from income to savings and back and forth. Want to spend $50,000 a year in retirement? Well, this means you need an investment portfolio worth $1,250,000 ($50,000/4%).

Want to spend $80,000 a year in retirement? Well, you would need an investment portfolio worth $2,000,000 ($80,000/4%).

Have only $500,000 saved for retirement? Well, this will only produce an income of $20,000/year in retirement ($500,000 x 4%).

Using this formula, you see that a successful retirement isn't some magical destination in a future shrouded in secrecy. Your retirement is a number. Reach that number and you can retire. You can also use this number to assess all along the way how close you are to your goal.

Designing Your Life on Your Terms: Aligning Priorities and Actions

What do you want your life to look like?

When I managed large teams, some of my direct reports were managers themselves. And when things would get tough with lots of high-stakes projects, I would ask them what their calendar looked like. That's because you can look at anyone's calendar and tell what their priorities are.

Priorities aren't what you say—they are what you actually do. Often, we end up with a lot of internal conflict and guilt because our actions don't match our truest priorities.

Want to prioritize your fitness? Great. If someone looked at your week, how often would they see you working out?

Want to prioritize spending quality time with your kids? Awesome. If someone looked at your week, how often would they see you spending unstructured time with your kids, just playing?

Want to prioritize the relationship with your significant other? Amazing. If someone looked at your week, how often would they see the two of you going on small adventures together?

Likewise, your spending and savings habits tell everyone what your priorities are. Remember, it's not what you say, it's what you actually do.

As kids, we are taught how to stand in straight lines. How to sit quietly and raise our hands. How to study for the standardized tests. How to get a good education so that we can get a good job.

Unfortunately, the downside of this behavior is that we tend to prioritize what others want us to do, what others want us to be like, rather than being able to tap into our own inner voices for what is important to us. We start to prioritize "fitting in" rather than embracing being different.

And unfortunately, "fitting in" these days often leads to a life of being broke like everyone else.

To become wealthy as an OT, I want you to start listening to this inner voice again.

To share a personal example, my corporate career started to take off at the same time that our OT private pay practice started to get busy.

We were living in an expensive neighborhood in NYC, so our rent was costly. Moreover, the price of two kids in daycare was more than most people's mortgage payment. Despite making a good living, we still felt like we were living paycheck to paycheck. Not to mention, things felt unstable, because I could lose my job at any time and clients could stop booking with our private pay practice. If these two things happened, we would be ruined. Things were a little stressful around our house!

At one point, we had some family in town, and my wife and I booked a hotel room in NYC for a night away for the first time since our son was born. The hotel room was large by NYC standards. And as we sat there looking at it, we imagined what life would be like if, instead of a big apartment, we lived in something the size of this hotel room.

We caught ourselves saying things like "We could have bunk beds over in that corner," and then "We could get some innovative storage solutions from IKEA and have the kids toys over in that corner. Instead of a dining room table taking up a lot of room, we should have something that folds up and is put away when we aren't eating." Through the simple act of talking and visualizing, we came to the conclusion that we needed to move out of our apartment. Our apartment wasn't huge, but it was nice and in an expensive neighborhood.

And so, we set about to downsize our apartment and move into a more affordable neighborhood. We found a one-bedroom apartment on the edge of Chinatown and the Lower East Side. The living room was large and long, and we put up a temporary wall at the far end where our kids' bunk beds and their IKEA storage went. We enrolled our kids into a good daycare in Chinatown. Our family of four lived in this one bedroom for over three years.

I bring this up because everyone thought we were absolutely crazy. Everyone around us had an opinion about how we should live. I received a huge promotion while we were living there. Our private pay practice got super busy.

Surely, being "successful" should come with all the outward signs of success? My boss couldn't understand why we still lived in a small one-bedroom apartment. But my wife and I were working on a bigger plan. And, for us, living in this small apartment was one of the best decisions we made. Here are a few of the highlights:

- We immediately cut our fixed expenses in half. That isn't a typo.

- Over the course of those three years, we paid off all our debt with the money we saved.

- Because our living expenses were so under control, we finally felt like we could breathe freely. We felt a massive reduction in stress.

- We put our kids into a lot of activities without regard to their cost because our fixed living expenses were so under control.

- We massively increased our retirement savings.

- With our expenses under control, we did prioritize date night. About three times a month, we went out on dates which did wonders for our marriage.

- We could walk our kids to their school, which massively cut down on commuting stress. This gave us back a ton more time in the morning and the evening.

- We started to both become a lot more successful at work and increased our income. I don't think this is a coincidence because our reduced stress allowed us to think more clearly and strategically with both our private pay practice and my corporate career.

Why do I tell you this story? Because many of the people who were critical of our life choices are still living paycheck to paycheck. If we had done only the things we were supposed to do, then we wouldn't have the freedom and flexibility we have today.

Becoming the "Strange" Millionaire: Bucking Conventional Wisdom

Becoming a wealthy OT may require you to be strange in your social circle. It will probably require you to make some choices that will cause some head turning by your peers. It requires you to buck conventional wisdom because conventional wisdom will keep you broke like everyone else.

We may think we are immune to the pressure of keeping up with the Joneses, but I've found over the years that often, we aren't as immune as we might think.

And that's because we've been indoctrinated from the beginning to define success based on material possessions. Because of this, we never take the time to question it. It becomes default behavior.

Here are some ideas to help you rethink normal:

- Instead of buying the biggest house you can afford, how about you buy the smallest house you can? You don't need a house with more bathrooms than occupants. You'll save money on the mortgage and utilities, and upkeep will be easier than for a larger house.
- Why not buy a duplex or triplex? Live on one side and rent out the others.
- Or buy a small townhouse when you first start working. Live there for five to seven years. When you finally,

absolutely, need more space, rent it out when you buy a larger place.

- There is nothing wrong with renting. You get flexibility to move easily compared to buying. And most people underestimate the cost of maintaining their home. A/Cs, gutters, and roofs need replacing, which costs thousands of dollars in addition to the time and stress of dealing with it. Renting can actually be cheaper and less stressful.
- Never buy a new car. Cars are a huge wealth trap. Buy a beater for cash and say goodbye to monthly car payments. Use that money for your retirement savings.

Reclaiming Your Financial Independence, Flexibility, and Freedom

You can fundamentally change the direction of your financial life through a few simple changes.

There is a lot of stress we experience because we make choices that aren't aligned with our highest priorities. This is especially true when it comes to our finances. Becoming a wealthy OT will require you to do some odd things. There is no way around it. Most people don't prioritize their financial future. Broke has become the new normal.

Therefore, if you're going to buck this trend, then it automatically places you on a different path—a path to reclaiming your financial independence, flexibility, and freedom.

Becoming a wealthy OT is within your reach. By shattering the millionaire myth, shifting your mindset from consumer to owner, and designing your life on your terms, you can create a future of financial independence and flexibility. It may require you to be strange in the eyes of others, but by embracing unconventional guidance, you'll break free from the new normal of being broke.

Your journey starts now. Armed with these strategies, you have the power to change your financial trajectory. Stay the course, prioritize your future, and watch your wealth grow. As an OT, you have what it takes to make this choice a reality.

CHAPTER FOUR

START INVESTING NOW - NOT LATER

"It's not about timing the market, but rather time in the market that matters."

– Peter Lynch

If you've read other personal finance books, the conventional advice given is typically as follows:

1. Do the equivalent of a proctology exam on your spending to figure out where your money is going.
2. Clip coupons, eat beans and rice, stop buying coffee, and start paying off your debt.
3. Once your debt is paid off, then start saving for retirement.

This advice isn't all bad, but it misses a few key things. Namely, it misses the following:

1. Most people are 100% intimidated about investing. Avoiding this until "some date in the future" doesn't help.
2. The major focus on paying off debt is good. However, it needs to be nuanced because, often, people are missing

out on a significant source of savings: their 401(k) employer match.

3. Investing takes years (or decades) to reap the benefits. We need to change our behavior today to make investing automatic, continuous, and a part of our life. We shouldn't wait for "someday." As Janet Daily said: "Someday is not a day of the week."

Personal finance is all about your behavior, mastering your psychology around money and, in many ways, "protecting yourself from yourself." That's why I prefer to do the opposite of most personal finance advice out there.

Start Building Your Investing Muscle Today

I want you to start investing first—right now, not tomorrow, not next week. *Today.*

Why? Because we need to start building your investing muscle. I don't care if you are investing $50 or $5. We need to build the habit of investing. That way, once you start getting a handle on your debt and spending, your accounts are already set up, already automated, and you can turn on the spigot of money flowing into your investing accounts without delay.

Intimidation is one of the biggest barriers I see for OTs when it comes to investing. Here's what happens:

1. They hear an alphabet soup of accounts, such as 401(k), 403(b), Roth IRA, HSA, etc., and are intimidated by what they all mean. It becomes one more "thing to research," and so they put it down for another day. The problem? That day rarely comes.
2. They are Intimidated by the account set up process: *How do I do this? Where do I go?*
3. They feel intimidated by choosing their first investment once they get the account set up.

The Just Right Challenge: Your Four-Account Investing Roadmap

I believe in the just right challenge when it comes to investing. If I tell you to do a thousand different things, you'll be overwhelmed and not take action.

If I tell you to just do four? Well, that's a lot easier to manage. And here are the four accounts you should set up by the end of this chapter:

1. Your 401(k)
2. HSA
3. A Roth IRA
4. A taxable brokerage account

That's it. That's all for right now. Now, let's talk about these accounts, what they mean, and how to open them.

401(k): The Powerhouse of Your Retirement Portfolio

A 401(k) is a special type of retirement account that employers offer their employees. Your 401(k) offers huge benefits, many of which people don't take advantage of, that makes this the top priority account that you need to open and start contributing to in order to build your wealth.

The government actually wants you to become wealthy and financially independent. In fact, Congress has loaded all sorts of benefits into 401(k)s that enable you to do just that.

Let's go over some of the amazing benefits your 401(k) offers you:

- **You get to invest your money pre-tax.** So what's the big deal with this? Well, would you rather invest $100 or $75? Which one do you think is going to be better? Obviously everyone would rather invest $100 instead of $75—it's a no brainer. That's exactly the impact investing your money pretax in a 401(k) has. When you invest pretax in your 401(k), you get to invest the full $100. If you'd invested on an "after tax" basis, then the IRS would take out their 25% in taxes (or whatever your tax bracket is) and you'd be left with only $75 to invest. Investing in your 401(k) automatically leads to a greater amount invested without you needing to do anything!

- **Your money grows tax deferred.** This is another huge benefit. Taxes are beyond the scope of this book, but I imagine you've heard terms like capital gains tax. In regular accounts, anytime you buy or sell securities, you face a potential tax bill. This tax bill will drag down your returns over time. In a 401(k), your portfolio grows tax free regardless of your trading activity, and you only pay taxes once you start taking distributions from your 401(k). This is absolutely massive and is the reason that your 401(k) is the first step in becoming financially independent.

- **You get an employer match.** The vast majority of employers offer a match for your 401(k) contributions up to a certain amount. The typical range is 4 to 6%. How does this work? Let's say you earn $80,000/year and your company matches the first 5% of your contributions. This means that when you contribute $4,000 to your 401(k) ($4,000 is 5% of $80,000), then your employer will match this $4,000 and contribute the same amount, dollar for dollar. Guess what? You've instantly doubled your $4,000 contribution to $8,000 by taking advantage of your match. And. . . you don't pay taxes on this $4,000 match, and it grows tax deferred as well. This type of "instant return" is (a) guaranteed and (b) impossible to find anywhere else.

The Employer Match: Your Golden Ticket to Wealth

Getting a match from your employer is like getting free money. Surprisingly, many people don't take advantage of this "free money." One of the biggest mistakes people make with their 401(k) is not contributing enough to get their full employer match.

In fact, a study in 2015 found that Americans miss out on a whopping $24 *billion* in unclaimed 401(k) matches each year![4] The "typical employee who doesn't maximize their employer's contribution misses out on an average of $1,336 in free money each year.

Let's do a quick exercise so you can see the power of getting your match. Let's suppose you make $80,000 a year and you receive a match up to 5% (assuming you start at age 25 and average 10% annual returns). Here's how much money you'd have with and without the match:

---

4 Financial Engines. (2015). Missing out: How much employer 401(k) matching contributions do employees leave on the table? Retrieved from https://content.money.com/wp-content/uploads/2015/05/financial-engines-401k-match-report-050615.pdf

Age	without match	with match
25	$ 4,400	$ 8,800
30	$ 30,862	$ 61,725
35	$ 74,125	$ 148,249
40	$ 143,799	$ 287,598
45	$ 256,010	$ 512,020
50	$ 436,727	$ 873,454
55	$ 727,774	$ 1,455,547
60	$1,172,087	$2,344,173

Taking the time to ensure you are getting the full match, if you are young enough, virtually guarantees that you will become financially independent. And we are just getting started.

If you weren't automatically enrolled into your 401(k) when you were hired, then reach out to Human Resources and ask them about the process to become enrolled and about the match. Complete the paperwork (which should be straightforward) and start contributing as much as you can (at least up to the match). Choose a target date fund with a year closest to when you plan to retire—typically around the year you turn 65. These funds automatically adjust their investment mix to become more conservative as you approach retirement, making them a simple, hands-off option for beginners. Note that I'm not covering 403(b)s in this chapter, but I do in Chapter 8. If you have a 403(b), instead of a 401(k), because you work at a nonprofit, then go ahead and make sure you are enrolled.

HSA: The Triple Tax Advantage for Your Health and Wealth

You are eligible to open an HSA account if you are in a High Deductible Health Plan (HDHP). If you aren't currently in an HDHP and don't have access to select one, then skip ahead. If not, then, you'll want to open an HSA.

An HSA is incredible because you get a triple tax benefit:

- Your contributions are pre-tax
- The growth of your investments is tax-free
- Your withdrawals for qualified medical expenses are tax-free

Unlike a Flexible Spending Account (FSA), an HSA rolls over each year, meaning that you don't have to use all the funds that year. Instead, it will keep growing if you have invested the funds.

If you have regular and predictable medical expenses, then using an FSA makes the most sense because it allows you to set aside pre-tax dollars to cover these costs. Unlike an HSA, which requires a high-deductible health plan (HDHP) and is more suited for saving and investing over the long term, an FSA is specifically designed for short-term medical expenses. With an FSA, you can access the full annual contribution amount at the start of the plan year, even if you haven't contributed the full amount yet. This makes it a practical option for covering known, recurring expenses like prescriptions, co-pays, or ongoing treatments. The real advantage to an HSA is leveraging the investment component. Yes, investing does carry risks which is why it is important to only invest money you don't need in the short-term. To take full advantage of the investment component of an HSA, you want to take the long-term buy-and-hold approach.

Action: If you have an HDHP, ask your Human Resources team if they have an employer-sponsored HSA. If they do, then enroll in that and pick your investment options. Again, target date funds are the simplest way to get started. If that isn't an option, then look for a broad index fund with a low expense ratio.

Here are a couple of popular, low-cost index funds:

- Vanguard Total Stock Market ETF (symbol VTI). This covers the entire U.S. stock market, including large-, mid-, small-, and micro-cap stocks. The expense ratio is only 0.03%.

- Vanguard S&P 500 ETF (symbol VOO). This tracks the performance of the 500 largest U.S. companies, representing about 80% of the total U.S. stock market. The expense ratio is also 0.03%.

If your employer doesn't offer an HSA but you are in an HDHP, then you can open one yourself through a service like Fidelity.

Roth IRA: The Tax-Free Growth and Withdrawal Advantage

I go into a lot more detail on all these different accounts in Chapter 8, but for now, you should know that a Roth IRA is a type of individual retirement account.

The good thing about a Roth IRA is that even though you contribute money after-tax, your growth is tax-free, and your withdrawals are tax-free as well, if you meet certain criteria. You must be at least 59.5 years old and have had the account longer than five years.

Not paying taxes on growth or withdrawals carry significant financial advantages that you'll want to maximize.

Go to Fidelity or Vanguard and open a Roth IRA. The account creation process is incredibly easy and takes 10 to 15 minutes. You'll set up automatic bank transfers and select your investment option. Again, make your life simple and just choose a target date fund. You can typically reduce account fees by opting to receive digital statements instead of paper. Set an amount you'd like to invest and make the contribution automatic. You'll learn more about this in later chapters, so for now, just choose something that gets you started. You'll be adjusting this amount as you work on your budget, paying off debt and increasing your income.

Brokerage Account: Your Flexible Investing Option

The first three accounts we talked about had significant tax advantages, and it was no accident we focused on those first. The US Government wants you to save for retirement and incentivizes you to do so through tax laws. You should take full advantage of the tax reduction efforts that have been signed into law.

However, all those tax advantaged accounts have their limits in terms of how much you can contribute. If you take advantage of those accounts and still have money left to invest, you'll do so in a regular brokerage account.

The money you contribute to a regular brokerage account is after-tax money and any gains you make, you'll pay taxes on when you sell. You have the most flexibility with a brokerage account (e.g. you can withdraw any time you want), but the flip side is that you pay taxes on any of your gains.

Like all investing, you want to take the long-term view—don't speculate and only invest money that you don't need for the next 5 to 10 years.

Open a brokerage account at Fidelity or Vanguard. To keep it simple and connected, I would suggest you open it at the same institution that you opened your Roth IRA. The account opening process is simple. Choose a small amount to contribute regularly right away, which you'll update as you work on your budget.

CHAPTER FIVE

BUILDING WEALTH FROM WHAT YOU ALREADY MAKE

> *"Do not save what is left after spending, but spend what is left after saving."*
>
> – Warren Buffett

Let's say that tomorrow you inherited $2,250,000! What would you do?

You'd probably immediately jump up and down and celebrate finally having some financial freedom! You'd feel a huge weight lift off your chest and finally be able to breathe without restriction. *Heck yes!*

After the initial excitement wore off, many of you would realize what a huge responsibility you've been blessed with. You'd want to make sure that you were good stewards of the money. You'd want to make sure you set yourself up for success so that this money would last. Heck, maybe it would even last so long you could pass some of it on to your kids or your favorite charity.

Now... Here comes the twist.

Let's assume that you earn $75,000/year as an OT.

Well, if the average OT works 30 years, then 30 years x $75,000/year = $2,250,000!

Reframing Your Earning Potential: An OT's Lifelong Journey

That's right, over your working lifetime you'll make $2,250,000! If you've got a spouse or partner making the same amount, then as a household you'll make $4.5 million!

Because we are earning this money in small increments over a long period of time, we never stop to think about the total amount of money we make. We don't approach our yearly income with the same steadfastness, seriousness, and responsibility that we would if we got it in a lump sum.

But the way to think about this is to say to yourself: "Over my lifetime I will make millions. If I want to become financially free, then I simply need to figure out how to keep more of what I'm already making."

You see, building wealth as an OTP is like cooking. You already have the raw ingredients (your income), you just need a different recipe (spending plan).

Designing Your Financial Roadmap: Goal-Directed Money Management

We can't get to our destination if we don't know our starting point.

I've met only a few people who enjoy budgeting. In fact, most people recoil at the idea because it seems incredibly restrictive. Instead, I like to recommend a conscious spending plan.

What is a conscious spending plan? It is being aware of where your money is going, what you value, and increasing spending on things you find meaningful and cutting out the rest.

The result? You won't feel like you are pinching pennies and instead will feel like you are living the high life, because your spending is aligned to what is meaningful to you.

But it all starts with better understanding your monthly cashflow.

What is cashflow? It is simply this:

Cashflow = Money In − Money Out

What is "Money In"? Well, "Money In" is simply all the forms of income you have coming in each month. This includes:

- Your income each month
- Your spouse/partner's income each month
- Any additional sources of income such as:
  - Side hustle income
  - Dividends or interest payments
  - Royalties
  - Rent received from investment properties
  - Child support, alimony, disability benefits

Likewise, "Money Out" is simply all the spending that is happening each month. This includes:

- Savings each month (emergency fund, retirement savings, short-term/long-terms savings, etc.)
- Fixed expenses (rent, mortgage, student loan payments, car payments, insurance, etc.)
- Variable expenses (food, entertainment, clothing, etc.)

Here's an example of how this comes together.

	"Money In"	
Income		Amount
	OT Monthly Salary	$6,000
	Partner's Monthly Salary	$5,000
	Additional Sources of Income	$0
	Monthly Gross Income	**$11,000**
	Federal Income Tax	-$1,250
	Social Security	-$682
	Medicare	-$160
	State Income Tax	-$550
	Total Estimated Taxes	**-$2,642**
	Total "Money In"	**$8,359**

	"Money Out"	
Savings		**Amount**
	Emergency fund	$100
	Down payment fund	$300
	Retirement	$300
	Total Savings	**$700**
Fixed Expenses		
	Rent	$1,400
	Childcare	$1,200
	Car payments	$280
	Student Loan payments	$1,132
	Insurance (healthcare, car, rental, etc.)	$500
	Total Fixed Expenses	**$4,512**

Variable Expenses		
	Food	$720
	Eating out	$200
	Entertainment	$200
	Utilities	$180
	Credit Card Payment	$150
	Gas	$200
	Clothing	$150
	Travel	$400
	Misc	$300
	Total Variable Expenses	**$2,500**
	Total "Money Out"	**$7,712**

Cashflow (Money In - Money Out)	**$647**

And now it is your turn, create your own template to calculate your monthly cashflow:

	"Money In"	
Income		Amount
	OT Monthly Salary	
	Partner's Monthly Salary	
	Additional Sources of Income	
	Monthly Gross Income	
	Federal Income Tax	
	Social Security	
	Medicare	
	State Income Tax	
	Total Estimated Taxes	
	Total "Money In"	

	"Money Out"	
Savings		Amount
	Emergency fund	
	Down payment fund	
	Retirement	
	Total Savings	
Fixed Expenses		
	Rent	
	Childcare	
	Car payments	
	Student Loan payments	
	Insurance (healthcare, car, rental, etc.)	
	Total Fixed Expenses	

Variable Expenses		
	Food	
	Eating out	
	Entertainment	
	Utilities	
	Credit Card Payment	
	Gas	
	Clothing	
	Travel	
	Misc	
	Total Variable Expenses	
	Total "Money Out"	

Cashflow (Money In - Money Out)	

Putting together your cashflow each month is the first step to understanding what's happening with your money.

Imagine you're working with a client who has a goal to improve their hand function after an injury. You wouldn't just start with random exercises and hope for the best. Instead, you begin with a thorough assessment, set specific, measurable goals, and develop a detailed treatment plan. This plan includes which exercises to perform, how often, and what adaptations or tools might be needed to achieve the best outcome. You monitor progress, adjust the plan as necessary, and ensure every action is purposeful toward the goal of improved hand function.

Now, think of understanding your cashflow in the same way. Your income is like your client's baseline ability. Your financial goals (saving for a house, retirement, or an emergency fund) are like the client-patient's recovery goals. Just as you wouldn't leave your client's progress to chance, you shouldn't leave your financial health to chance either.

The first time you look at your cashflow will take you the longest. Here's what you need to do:

- Collect all the sources of your income.
- Go through the past three to four months of your bank statements and credit card statements to determine where and how much you've been spending.

Fortunately, there are some automatic options that simplify the process significantly:

- Most online banking platforms will automatically categorize your income and expenses for you. If you have a simple financial picture (e.g. not a lot of different accounts) then this is where I'd start.
- If you have multiple accounts that all need to be consolidated into one picture (or your bank doesn't offer tools), then you can use an online tool like You Need A Budget (YNAB), EveryDollar, or Personal Capital.

The key is to not just look at one month's worth, but to go back and look at the last three to six months of monthly cashflows. This helps smooth out some of the big one-time expenses (such as a big trip, holiday spending, etc.) and the natural fluctuations that exist with the "variable" category.

Important: Many people are naturally anxious to investigate the details of where they are spending their money. In fact, it is common to have an avoidance behavior when it comes to checking your bank account balance, let alone taking a fresh look at your spending. So, I recommend you approach this task from a place of curiosity, not judgement. The past is the past. You can't change it, but you can bring greater awareness to your spending and make a plan for the future.

Mindfully Examining Your Spending Patterns

As you are reviewing the last three to six months, I want you to ask the following questions:

1. **What are my core values?** Before diving into the numbers, it's crucial to define what matters most. Is it family, health, education, travel, or perhaps giving back to the community?

2. **Does my spending reflect my values?** Look at the top three to five expenses and see if they directly support what you cherish most in life.

3. **What brings me joy and fulfillment?** Identify which purchases over the last few months have contributed to genuine happiness and a sense of well-being.

4. **Am I investing in my future?** Consider whether a portion of your spending is going toward long-term goals, such as retirement, a home purchase, or further education.

5. **What expenses did I forget about shortly after making them?** Recognize spending that didn't leave a lasting impact or contribute to your happiness.

6. **How does my spending impact my stress levels and mental health?** Reflect on whether financial decisions are causing stress or if they're aligned with a healthy, balanced lifestyle.

7. **Am I spending on necessities or wants?** Distinguish between what you truly need and what you desire as a luxury or convenience.

8. **Could I have enjoyed a similar experience for less?** Think about whether there were opportunities to save money while still enjoying the essence of what you value (e.g., cooking a gourmet meal at home vs. dining out).

9. **What spending habits would I like to change?** Identify specific behaviors you want to adjust to better align with your values and financial goals.

10. **How can I make more room for the things that matter most?** Strategize ways to reduce or eliminate spending in areas that are less important to you to free up resources for more meaningful expenditures.

11. **What are my financial goals for the next year, and how does my current spending support these goals?** Ensure your spending is not just about immediate gratification but also about reaching your future objectives.

12. **How does my spending affect my relationships?** Consider whether your financial habits are enriching or straining your connections with loved ones.

13. **What sacrifices am I willing to make to live more in line with my values?** Reflect on areas you're willing to cut back on to fund the aspects of life you truly value.

14. **How do I feel when I make a purchase?** Pay attention to your emotions during and after making a purchase to understand your spending triggers better.

15. **What lessons have I learned from reviewing my past spending, and how can I apply them moving forward?** Use your insights to make more informed, value-aligned decisions in the future.

Prioritizing Your Financial Well-Being: Paying Yourself First With a 50-30-20 Plan

After looking at your monthly cashflow, the natural question is "what now?" This is where having a benchmark in mind is important.

For most people, the following happens each month:

1. They get their paychecks deposited
2. Rent or mortgage gets taken out
3. Loan payments get made
4. Car payments get made
5. Gas is bought to put in the car
6. Food is bought
7. The pattern repeats with other bills and daily expenses... Finally, at the end of the month, any money that is left-over is "saved" for our future

We pay everyone else first, and then we pay ourselves with what's left. The key to building wealth is to flip this around and pay yourself first.

It requires a fundamental mindset shift: *Instead of saving what's left after spending, we spend what's left after saving.*

This is a 180-degree shift from what you are probably doing today (along with the vast majority of the population).

We need to pay ourselves first for a few reasons:

- The average length of retirement is 11,000 days. This is 11,000 days of expenses that our retirement portfolio needs to cover. If we don't prioritize our own savings and investing, then we simply won't be prepared.
- It is natural (and expected!) that our spending starts to match our earnings. If we have $100 to spend, we will spend $100. Paying yourself first ensures you are saving $20 first so you only spend $80.
- Paying yourself first means that you can spend the remainder without guilt. You know you are on the right track.

Your goals are going to be specific to you. How soon you want to retire, your short-term goals, etc. are specific to you.

A great place to start is to think about your spending in categories as a percentage of your income. And the 50-

30-20 plan is popular in personal finance circles because it emphasizes savings and is simple to understand. Put simply, the 50-30-20 plans says:

- 50% of your income goes to needs (fixed expenses)
- 30% of your income goes to wants (variable expenses)
- 20% of your income goes to savings/investing

So, how does your cashflow align to this simple prescription? Go back to your cashflow analysis and calculate it as a percentage of your income.

Let's do this with the example provided in the previous section. I will focus on the net income (after taxes).

- This couple had a monthly net income of $8,359. According to the 50-30-20 plan:
  - 50% of $8,359 should be spent on fixed expenses. This equates to $4,179.5/month.
  - 30% of $8,359 should be spent on variable expenses. This equates to $2,507.7/month.
  - 20% of $8,359 should be spent on savings/investing. This equates to $1,671.8.

So how does this hypothetical couple stack up with their actual spending? The table below summarizes it:

	Benchmark Spending	Actual Spending	Benchmark %	Actual %
Fixed	$4,179	$4,512	50%	53%
Variable	$2,508	$2,500	30%	28%
Savings	$1,672	$1,609	20%	19%

Given this couple had an extra $647/month in cashflow, I put that in the savings category as it was extra money each month they could save or use to pay off their debt.

Evaluating Your Financial Health: A Holistic Assessment

From this table we can draw a few conclusions:

- Overall, they are doing a great job.
- They probably need to up their savings for their emergency fund, since $100/month isn't much.
- But, their fixed expenses are a little higher than they should be. They are spending $4,512 instead of $4,179. Out of the $4,512, they are spending $1,412/month between car payments and student loans. This is the primary place I would look to pay off debt (using the $647/month of cashflow) so they can reduce this down in short order.

- Over time, I want to see the category of "cars + student loans" reduced to 0. This will free up $1,412/month for saving and investing.

How does your current spending stack up against these percentages? Go ahead and fill out this table:

	Benchmark %	My %
Fixed	50%	
Variable	30%	
Savings	20%	

Once you have these percentages filled out, ask yourself the following questions:

- Are your fixed expenses aligned with your income?
- Are your variable expenses aligned with your income?
- Are you paying yourself first each month?

Assessing Your Cashflow and Developing a Plan

When you look at your monthly cashflow, there are only three possible outcomes:

1. *Cashflow > 0*

   This means that your monthly income is greater than your monthly expenses. The implication here is that you have extra money to either save more or pay off debt faster.

2. *Cashflow = 0*

   This means that you are spending exactly the same amount you make each month.

3. *Cashflow < 0*

   This means that your income doesn't cover your expenses each month and that you are likely living on credit cards to fund your lifestyle.

Let's address #3 first. If you are experiencing negative cashflow each month, then it simply means your current lifestyle is unsustainable. Why? Because each month you are spending more than you make. That means that, each month, you are going more and more debt. This is a precarious situation to be in, and we need to fix this as soon as possible to lessen the long-term consequences.

When you find yourself in a hole, the most important thing to do is stop digging. Regardless of which situation you are in, we want to ask yourself the following:

- What expenses can you eliminate right away? The variable expense category is easier to change right away.
  - Look at ongoing subscriptions and fees where you can immediately reduce.

- How can you reduce your food budget? Cook more meals at home. Bring your lunch to work.

- Take a pause from purchasing new things. Stopping impulse purchases can be hard, but over time it adds up. In an age of "add to cart," it is super easy to overspend in this category. My suggestion? Institute one day per week when you make purchases online. During the week, when you get the urge to buy something online, write it down on the list for the "weekly" purchase. Then, once a week, review the list and discern if (a) you really need it and (b) if it fits within your budget.

- Look at your fixed expenses and see if there are some big moves you can make. Most people spend the most on a few categories: rent/mortgage, childcare, cars, and loan repayments.

  - **Rent:** If you are renting, can you downsize to a cheaper place the next time your lease is up? Can you avoid purchasing a home until you've paid off some of your debt? If you do purchase, can you save up a larger down payment to reduce your monthly expenses? Could you purchase a duplex, live in one side, and rent out the other? Could you buy a townhouse (usually cheaper) and live in that for three to five years while you get a handle on your finances?

- **Mortgage:** If you own your home, it can be tougher to reduce your monthly expenses. Unfortunately, many people buy a house that is way too expensive relative to their income. That's because banks and mortgage brokers will want to put you in the most expensive home possible to maximize their commission and the loan you take out. Don't be persuaded by being "qualified" for a certain loan amount. The percentages that banks and brokers use for that calculation will keep you struggling financially. Aim to purchase a home that is no more than 2–2.5 times your annual income.

- **Childcare:** The cost of daycare has gotten out of control. What choices are available in your area? Daycare in expensive neighborhoods will be more expensive than their counterparts across town. But, it doesn't always mean the quality is lower (just their fixed expenses like rent may be lower so they can charge less). Can you find a great alternative that is more affordable? Is there a creative solution involving family members who are local?

- **Cars and student loan repayments:** We cover this in upcoming chapters.

Charting Your Course to Financial Freedom: An OT's Action Plan

Let's recall the cashflow formula:

$$Cashflow = Money\ In - Money\ Out$$

We want to do two things at once:

- Increase "Money In"
- Decrease the fixed and variable "Money Out" so we have more money for savings/investing

This is how you become financially free.

I want to be clear about something. I am actually a big fan of spending money. And I'm a big fan of you spending money as well.

I am not at all saying you should live under a rock, eat ramen every day, and be the most boring person in the room.

The reality is that most of the money we spend is going toward debt payments. The money is going toward:

- Mortgage payments
- Car payments
- Credit card bills
- Student loans, etc.

Think about it this way: how are you supposed to have the money to invest if all the money you have is being spent toward paying someone else (banks, etc.)?

Your income is your biggest wealth-building machine. It is time to stop paying others and start paying yourself.

And that's what we are going to cover in the next few chapters:

- The real cost of debt (Chapter 6)
- How to get out of debt (Chapter 7)
- How to invest your money (Chapter 8)
- How to increase your income (Chapter 9)

Let's dive in!

CHAPTER SIX

THE DEBT TRAP: UNDERSTANDING THE TRUE COST OF BORROWED MONEY

"Debt is like any other trap, easy enough to get into, but hard enough to get out of."

– Michelle Singletary

By the end of this chapter, I want you to have a new outlook on debt.

When we first start working, we immediately think along these lines: *Oh, what can I afford?* And then, when we start getting income increases, we naturally think: *Oh, I got a raise, what can I buy?*

Most of the time, we aren't making our purchases by buying an item outright. Instead, we set ourselves up for monthly payments and we pay it off over time.

We do this with all sorts of things:

- We don't pay our tuition in full but take out loans that we repay over time.
- We don't buy a car with cash but instead finance it with monthly payments.
- Those dinners out? Those new clothes for work? Those go on a credit card on which we make minimum payments.
- Big holiday purchases? Well, we don't have the cash, so they also go on a credit card, and we pay them back over time.
- An unexpected emergency? That goes on a credit card, or we take out a home equity line of credit and add it to our mortgage.

And when we do this, our instinct when looking at buying something is not: "Can I afford this?" but rather: "Can I afford the monthly payments?" The problem is that those monthly payments quickly add up and you'll pay more in the long-term due to the interest you are paying.

OTs Beware: How Monthly Payments Keep You Stressed and Broke

I hope I've built up some goodwill by this point, so I'm going to be uncharacteristically blunt: your monthly payments will keep you stressed out about money, and you'll never attain financial freedom.

I don't want you to think you are alone here. In our culture, it is deeply embedded to eat up all our income with purchases. The famous singer Rihanna was on the verge of bankruptcy and sued her accountant. In response to the suit, the accountant wrote: "Was it really necessary to tell her that if you spend money on things, you will end up with things and not money?"

It is obvious when others are doing it, but often we don't apply the same awareness to our own spending. In fact, having monthly payments conceals two key facets of which I want you to be aware:

1. The total cost of all those monthly payments
2. The missed opportunity cost of those monthly payments

What's the Total Cost?

When we finance something (tuition, cars, purchases on credit cards, etc.) we get into a weird mirage where we only consider whether or not we can afford the monthly payments rather than the total cost.

We say: "Oh, this car only costs $279/month. I can make those payments," or "I'll pay for the new iPhone on an installment plan. It's only an extra $25/month." Or we even say: "I can afford to make the minimum payment on my credit card. Let me just put this next purchase on it. After all, it builds my credit."

This is exactly how banks and lenders want you to behave. The more, and longer, you pay the banks and lenders the more money *they* make and the less *you* will have.

Uncovering the Hidden Costs of Financing

To illustrate, let's take a car as an example. If you buy a car for $28,000 and finance it over five years at 7% interest rate (the rate will depend on where interest rates are and your credit score), then the total cost of the car isn't $28,000 but rather $33,349.80!

	Loan Amount	Interest Rate	Term	Monthly Payment	Total Interest Paid	Total Cost of Loan
Car	$28,000	7%	5 years	$555.83	$5,349.80	$33,349.80

In total, you've spent an extra $5,350 on the car! And this $5,350 is huge considering that most Americans have less than $1,000 saved for emergencies.[5] It is no wonder—we are paying all our money to banks and lenders!

---

5 Bankrate. (2023). More than half of Americans couldn't cover a $1,000 emergency expense. Retrieved from https://www.bankrate.com/banking/savings/financial-security-january-2023/

Not to mention, cars almost always depreciate over time. So, in five years you won't be able to sell the car for $33,459 or even $28,000. It will likely be worth about 40% less than what you paid for it (about $16,800).

Credit cards are even worse. There are two major problems with credit cards:

- The interest rates are astronomical: often in the 15–29.99% range.
- The "minimum monthly payment" greatly conceals the true cost.

Let's take a simple example. Let's assume you owe $6,500 on your credit card with an annual interest rate of 20%. And your credit card requires you to pay a minimum of 2% of the balance or $25, whichever is higher (common terms).

Well, you get your monthly bill, and it tells you that you only owe $130/month which you immediately think: *Awesome, I can do that!*

Due to a combination of the high interest rate and relatively low monthly payment, this $6,500 will take a whopping 15 years and 4 months to pay off! And you'll pay $8,600 in interest—more than the original balance!

Balance	Interest Rate	Minimum Payment Calculation	Starting Minimum Payment	Time to Pay Off	Total Interest Paid	Total Cost
$6,500	20%	2% of balance or $25, whichever is higher	$130	15 years and 4 months	$8,600	$15,100

In the credit card example above, the initial minimum payment is $130/month.

The Price of Debt for OTs: The Staggering Cost of Debt-Fueled Spending

What would happen if you didn't have credit card debt and, instead, decided to invest $130/month for 15 years and 4 months?

Well, using an average return of 10% (historical stock market returns), then you'd have a portfolio worth over $54k after 15 years!

I don't know about you, but I'd much rather have $54k in 15 years instead of some item I bought 15 years ago that I (a) probably no longer use and (b) can't even find!

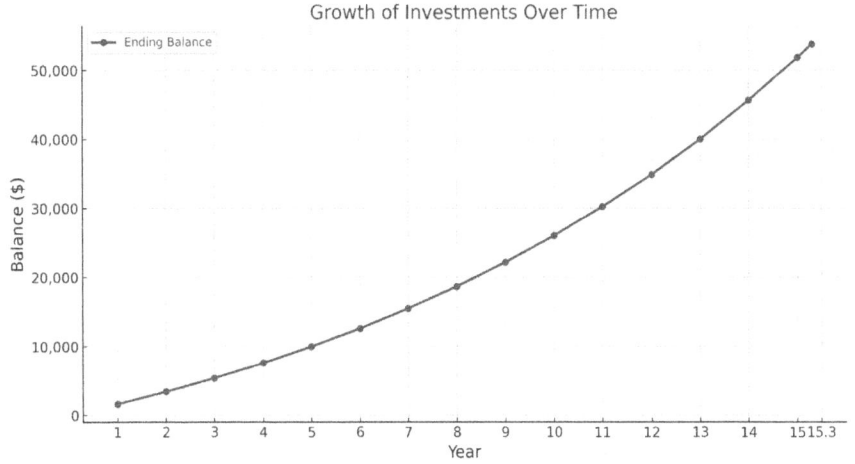

Drowning in Debt: Why OTs Struggle to Get Ahead Financially

There is nothing more frustrating and demotivating than looking at your cashflow at the end of the month and realizing that a big percentage of your income went to pay for things that you bought years ago.

Between the total cost of debt + the missed opportunity costs, it is clear that debt is going to always be a huge strain in getting ahead financially.

Until you pay off your debt, it will always feel like you are in a leaky ship. No amount of throwing water over the side with a pail will get you ahead. We have to fix the leak at its source.

Navigating the Debt Landscape: From Secured Loans to Sky-High Interest

Before going further, let's talk about all the different types of debt that are out there.

Secured vs. Unsecured Debt

Secured Debt

- **Definition:** Secured debt is backed by collateral. This means if you fail to repay the loan, the lender has the right to take the asset used as collateral to recover their funds.
- **Key Characteristic:** Because these loans are less risky for lenders (thanks to the collateral), they typically come with lower interest rates.
- **Examples:** Mortgages and auto loans are classic examples of secured debt. In the case of a mortgage, the house is the collateral. For an auto loan, it's the vehicle.

Unsecured Debt

- **Definition:** Unsecured debt does not require any collateral. If you default on an unsecured loan, the lender doesn't have an immediate right to any specific asset, although they can take other actions to recoup their money, such as suing you or hiring a collection agency.

- **Key Characteristic:** Higher risk for lenders translates to higher interest rates for borrowers compared to secured loans.
- **Examples:** Credit cards and personal loans are common forms of unsecured debt.

Student Loans: A Special Case

- Student loans are a bit of an anomaly. They're considered unsecured because you don't have to put up collateral to get them. However, unlike most other unsecured debts, it's notoriously difficult to discharge them in bankruptcy. This unique protection for lenders is why student loans can have relatively low interest rates compared to other unsecured debts, especially federal student loans which come with additional benefits and protections.

The Hierarchy of Debt for OTs: Ranking Loans from Best to Worst

Interest rates can vary widely based on factors like the type of loan, your credit score, and market conditions. However, here's a general ranking from lower to higher interest rates:

1. Secured Loans

- **Mortgages:** Often the lowest interest rates because they are long-term loans secured by real estate.

- **Auto Loans**: Rates are generally low but higher than mortgages due to the depreciating value of the vehicle.

2. Student Loans

- **Federal Student Loans**: Typically have lower interest rates and more flexible repayment options.
- **Private Student Loans**: Rates can vary, sometimes approaching unsecured personal loan rates, depending on the lender and your credit.

3. Unsecured Loans

- **Personal Loans**: Interest rates can vary widely. Those with excellent credit may get rates comparable to secured loans, but rates can be much higher for those with average or poor credit.
- **Credit Cards**: Usually carry the highest interest rates. Rates can be significantly higher for those with lower credit scores or for certain types of cards (like rewards cards).

The Great Debate for OTs: Is There Such a Thing as "Good" Debt?

So, is all debt bad? No, not necessarily. Some debt can be good, especially when used strategically.

The key question to ask yourself about the debt is the following: "Is the underlying thing I bought with debt going to increase in value?"

Going down the road of financial freedom means buying things that will increase in value over time rather than items that decline in value.

So, let's apply this filter to the above-mentioned types of debt and underlying assets:

Type of Debt	Underlying Asset	Increases in Value?
Mortgage	Home	Possibly, but not guaranteed
Auto Loan	Car	No, depreciates with time
Student Loan	Education	Not applicable (intangible asset)
Credit Card	Consumer Goods	No, generally depreciates quickly
Personal Loan	Varied	Depends on use (often no)

From the above table, pretty much the only type of "good" debt is a mortgage (but that comes with many caveats). The other types of debt (auto, credit card, personal loans) are just bad types of debt. They are expensive, and the underlying asset will decline over time. You've got a double whammy there.

You are paying *more* for the privilege of owning something that will be worth less and less over time. That's a pretty bad deal.

So, what about student loans? Are they "good" or "bad"?

OT Student Loans: The Double-Edged Sword of Financing Your Future

Tuition has been steadily increasing, but the common wisdom has been that taking out student loans is a path to economic security and higher earning potential.

Historically, this has been true. But in the last 15 to 20 years, tuition at OT schools has rapidly outpaced inflation. OT graduates now come out of school with an almost crippling level of student loan debt compared to their average salaries.

I'll dive into OT student loans specifically in an upcoming chapter, but suffice to say, I recommend you pay off your OT student loans as quickly as possible.

Escaping the Debt Trap: Proven Strategies for OTs to Accelerate Their Journey to Freedom

When You Find Yourself in a Hole, Stop Digging

Freeing up your monthly income from debt is the key to building financial freedom.

So, we must get out of debt.

I'm going to give you some tools for paying off your debt faster. Before I do, though, we must ensure that we set you up for success. What that means, simply, is: going forward stop taking out new debt:

- Keep the credit card in your sock draw at home so you can't use it
- Don't take out any new personal loans
- Keep driving your existing car, rather than buying a new one

Paying off your debt quickly does no good if you replace it with new debt. Breathing room and financial freedom start with freeing up your money each month to start working for you.

Understand Your Current Debt Situation

The first step of getting out of debt is thoroughly understanding your current debt situation. To accomplish that, take some time and write down the following:

- Loan ID (if you haven't consolidated your student loans, then you'll have lots of smaller loans adding up to the big total)
- Loan type (student loan, credit card, car loan, mortgage, etc.)
- Lender/Servicers name
- Current balance
- Interest rate
- Monthly payment
- Remaining years (for credit card put N/A)

Here's an example of what this would look like:

Loan ID	Loan Type	Lender's Name
Federal 1 (Subsidized)	Student Loan	Great Lakes
Federal 2 (Unsubsidized)	Student Loan	FedLoan Servicing
Federal 3 (Subsidized)	Student Loan	Nelnet
Federal 4 (Unsubsidized)	Student Loan	Navient
Private 1	Student Loan	Sallie Mae
Private 2	Student Loan	Discover Student Loans
Car Loan	Auto Loan	Chase Auto Finance
Credit Card	Credit Card	Capital One Quicksilver
Mortgage	Mortgage	Wells Fargo

Table continues on next page...

Current Balance	Interest Rate	Monthly Payment	Remaining Years
$20,000	4.5%	$207	10
$30,000	5.0%	$318	10
$15,000	4.5%	$155	10
$15,000	5.0%	$159	10
$10,000	7.0%	$116	10
$15,000	7.5%	$177	10
$15,000	4.5%	$280	5
$5,000	18.99%	$150	N/A
$250,000	6.0%	$1,499[6]	28

Going forward, our focus is going to be on non-mortgage-related debt. This is because mortgage debt is typically longer term, has a lower interest rate, and has an asset behind it that could appreciate. We will get the most bang for our buck by focusing on the non-mortgage-related debt.

---

[6] Note: taxes and home insurance are excluded from the mortgage amount as those aren't debts.

Avalanche vs Snowball: Choosing Your Path to Pay Off Your OT Debt

If you keep making the regular minimum monthly payments, then it is impossible to pay off your debt faster.

The only way to speed up is to make extra payments. And the question is: "Is there a strategy to making extra payments?"

And the answer is *yes*! There are two popular strategies you can choose between:

1. The avalanche method
2. The snowball method

Imagine you're trying to stop an avalanche from getting bigger. You'd tackle the biggest threat first, right? The avalanche method works similarly with debt. You list all your debts from the highest interest rate to the lowest. You pay the minimum on all your debts but focus any extra money you have on the debt with the highest interest rate. Once that's paid off, you move to the next highest interest rate, and so on. This method is like stopping the most dangerous parts of the avalanche first, saving you the most money in interest over time.

Using the avalanche method, this would be your order of priority in the previous example, with debts listed from highest interest rate to lowest:

Priority	Loan ID	Loan Type	Lender's Name	Current Balance	Interest Rate	Monthly Payment
1	Credit Card	Credit Card	Capital One Quicksilver	$5,000	18.99%	$150
2	Private 2	Student Loan	Discover Student Loans	$15,000	7.5%	$177
3	Private 1	Student Loan	Sallie Mae	$10,000	7.0%	$116
4	Federal 2 (Un-subsidized)	Student Loan	FedLoan Servicing	$30,000	5.0%	$318
5	Federal 4 (Un-subsidized)	Student Loan	Navient	$15,000	5.0%	$159
6	Federal 1 (Subsidized)	Student Loan	Great Lakes	$20,000	4.5%	$207
7	Federal 3 (Subsidized)	Student Loan	Nelnet	$15,000	4.5%	$155
8	Car Loan	Auto Loan	Chase Auto Finance	$15,000	4.5%	$280

So, in this example, any extra money you have would go toward paying off your credit card first (18.99% interest rate), and then once you've paid off your credit card entirely, you'd start making extra payments on the $15,000 "Private 2" student loan (7.5% interest rate).

Now, think about making a snowball. You start small and, as you roll it in the snow, it gets bigger. The snowball method for paying off debt starts with your smallest debt. You pay the minimum on all your debts and put any extra money toward the smallest debt until it's gone. Then, you take the money you were putting toward that debt and add it to the minimum payment on the next smallest debt, making the payment "snowball" bigger and bigger as you go. This method gives you quick wins, which can be motivating to keep going.

In the snowball method, this would be your order of priority in the example, listed from lowest loan balance to highest:

Priority	Loan ID	Loan Type	Lender's Name	Current Balance	Interest Rate	Monthly Payment
1	Credit Card	Credit Card	Capital One Quicksilver	$5,000	18.99%	$150
2	Private 1	Student Loan	Sallie Mae	$10,000	7.0%	$116
3	Private 2	Student Loan	Discover Student Loans	$15,000	7.5%	$177
4	Federal 3 (Subsidized)	Student Loan	Nelnet	$15,000	4.5%	$155
5	Federal 4 (Unsubsidized)	Student Loan	Navient	$15,000	5.0%	$159
6	Car Loan	Auto Loan	Chase Auto Finance	$15,000	4.5%	$280
7	Federal 1 (Subsidized)	Student Loan	Great Lakes	$20,000	4.5%	$207
8	Federal 2 (Unsubsidized)	Student Loan	FedLoan Servicing	$30,000	5.0%	$318

In this example, any extra money you have would go toward paying off your credit card first ($5,000 balance) and then once you've paid off your credit card entirely, you'd start making extra payments on "Private 1" student loan ($10,000 balance).

Which one should you use? The avalanche method will save you more money in the long run, because you are paying off the higher interest loans first. However, I often find that people get demotivated over time, which is where the snowball method shines. It can be rewarding to see loans get paid off, providing motivation to keep going.

From Overwhelmed to In Control: Crafting Your Personalized OT Debt-Freedom Plan

At this point, I wouldn't blame you for feeling overwhelmed. After all, once we start writing down our cashflows and our debt, it can honestly be quite scary. And it is all too easy for this to lead to avoidance, analysis paralysis, guilt, and shame.

There is a powerful reframe for your current situation. You have an amazing opportunity in front of you. You are learning about this *today* and you have the opportunity to put a plan in place *right now*. That is a lot better than if you learned about personal finance ten years from now. Or heck—never at all.

So yes, it can be overwhelming, but remember these wise words of Desmond Tutu: "There is only one way to eat an elephant: a bite at a time."

To recap, at this stage you understand:

- How much money you have coming in and out each month and your overall cashflow;
- The total cost of having debt (not just the monthly payments) and the missed opportunity cost (from not having extra cashflow to invest for your future);
- All your debts (excluding mortgage) listed out and prioritized either for the avalanche method or the snowball method;

It is now time to bring things together and come up with a plan for how you'll get out of debt faster. Changes are necessary because, in the words of Tony Robbins: "If you do what you've always done, you'll get what you've always gotten."

By now you know that to pay extra toward your debt, we need to somehow find extra money. There are many laws of the universe, but one of the unwritten ones is that money typically doesn't magically appear. However, we can go through our expenses and find places to optimize our spending.

Trimming the Fat: How OTs Can Slash Expenses to Supercharge Debt Repayment

See, there are only two ways for you to get more money to pay extra on your debt:

1. Reduce your monthly expenses, so you have more money to pay toward your debt
2. Increase your monthly income, so you have extra money to pay toward your debt

That's it—reduce your monthly expenses or increase your monthly income.

My preferred option is a combination of these two options. By combining both, you dramatically increase the time to pay off your debt and start building financial freedom. Plus, once you are debt-free, you have even more money to invest as you've raised the floor on your income.

To make this plan a reality, let's revisit the couple from the previous chapter. Remember, this is their monthly cashflow picture:

	"Money In"	
Income		Amount
	OT monthly salary	$6,000
	Partner's monthly salary	$5,000
	Additional sources of income	$0
	Monthly Gross Income	**$11,000**
	Federal income tax	-$1,250
	Social Security	-$682
	Medicare	-$160
	State income tax	-$550
	Total Estimated Taxes	**-$2,642**
	Total "Money In"	**$8,359**

	"Money Out"	
Savings		Amount
	Emergency fund	$100
	Down payment fund	$300
	Retirement	$300
	Total Savings	**$700**
Fixed Expenses		
	Rent	$1,400
	Childcare	$1,200
	Car payments	$280
	Student loan payments	$1,132
	Insurance (healthcare, car, rental, etc.)	$500
	Total Fixed Expenses	**$4,512**

Variable Expenses		
	Food	$720
	Eating out	$200
	Entertainment	$200
	Utilities	$180
	Credit card payment	$150
	Gas	$200
	Clothing	$150
	Travel	$400
	Misc	$300
	Total Variable Expenses	**$2,500**
	Total "Money Out"	**$7,712**
	Cashflow (Money In - Money Out)	**$647**

And here is their debt:

Priority	Loan ID	Loan Type	Lender's Name	Current Balance	Interest Rate	Monthly Payment
1	Credit Card	Credit Card	Capital One Quicksilver	$5,000	18.99%	$150
2	Private 1	Student Loan	Sallie Mae	$10,000	7.0%	$116
3	Private 2	Student Loan	Discover Student Loans	$15,000	7.5%	$177
4	Federal 3 (Subsidized)	Student Loan	Nelnet	$15,000	4.5%	$155
5	Federal 4 (Unsubsidized)	Student Loan	Navient	$15,000	5.0%	$159
6	Car Loan	Auto Loan	Chase Auto Finance	$15,000	4.5%	$280
7	Federal 1 (Subsidized)	Student Loan	Great Lakes	$20,000	4.5%	$207
8	Federal 2 (Unsubsidized)	Student Loan	FedLoan Servicing	$30,000	5.0%	$318
	Total			$125,000		$1,562

Here are some practical things this couple can do to pay more toward their debt:

1. They have cashflow of $647/month that can immediately be used to make extra payments.
2. Pause saving for a down payment on a home. The focus should be getting out of debt, not taking on new debt. This frees up another $300/month.
3. Reduce eating out to save another $100/month.
4. Reduce entertainment by $50/month.
5. Reduce travel from $400/month to $100/month. This is a temporary sacrifice to save another $300/month.
6. Either negotiate a rent decrease or move to a different home/apartment to save another $200/month.

Combined, the above actions mean they can start putting an extra $1,597/month toward their debt!

Remember how I said that a combination of earning more and reducing your expenses was an unbeatable combination? Well, the OT in this scenario decides to leverage her skills by seeing clients privately on the side on a part-time basis. Her practice is a cash-based provider (I cover this in Chapter 9), and she charges $100/session. Because she's starting part-time, she only sees three clients a week to keep her schedule manageable. This allows her to earn an extra $1,200/month, which is approximately $800/month after taxes.

All told, reducing their expenses and increasing their income allows them to pay an extra $2,397/month to their debt. The couple decides to follow the snowball method to reduce their debt, so they start paying extra on their credit card, the debt with the lowest balance.

In roughly two months their $5,000 credit card is paid off! After paying off their credit card, they have an extra $150/month to add to the $2,397/month in extra payments (so a total of $2,547/month—this also shows how your payments snowball!)

After paying off the credit card, they pay an extra $2,547/month toward Private Loan 1 (balance of $10k). It will take them approximately four months to pay off this loan.

After paying off $15k of debt in six months, they are starting to feel like they are getting some traction. They keep going, and now their snowball amount increases to $2,663. Note that, now that Private Loan 1 is paid off, they can use that monthly payment to increase the extra they can pay each month.

They move onto the next loan with the highest balance Private Loan 2 ($15k balance) and are able to pay this off in less than six months. They keep doing this until they are on their last loan ($30k, Federal 2, unsubsidized), by which time their extra monthly payments total $3,641.

Following this strategy, they will be debt free in about three years! They will also have saved tens of thousands in interest that wouldn't otherwise have gone to banks.

But there is another benefit that is absolutely huge—their overall financial situation. Remember, they simplified their life, decreased their expenses, and increased their income. Once they don't have those debt payments, they have this financial picture:

- $0 toward debt payments each month
- An extra $4,000/month (due to no debt payments, a decrease in expenses, and an increase in income)
- They will be millionaires in about 13.5 years if they invest $3k/month

Does this require some sacrifice? Absolutely, there is no way around it.

Before, though, all their money each month was going to paying other people. By getting control of their debt, their expenses, and increasing their income, they've taken control of their financial life, so they no longer feel out of control. And they now have something that is proven again and again to increase happiness: choices.

If we want more choices (which I think we all do), then putting in place a plan to reduce your debt as quickly as possible is absolutely the first step.

We've covered a lot of ground in this chapter. We've unmasked the true cost of debt, explored the different types of loans, and talked about the importance of creating a personalized debt-freedom plan. I know it can feel overwhelming at first, but remember, you're not alone in this. Millions of people who have achieved financial freedom started in similar places to where you are today.

The key is to take action, one step at a time. Start by conducting your debt audit and choosing your debt payoff strategy. Then look for ways to trim your expenses and boost your income. Every extra dollar you can throw at your debt will bring you closer to your goal. And don't forget to celebrate your progress along the way! Each debt you eliminate is a major victory worth acknowledging.

As Occupational Therapists, you are no stranger to hard work and dedication. You pour your heart into helping our clients overcome challenges and reach their full potential. Now, it's time to apply that same level of commitment to your own financial well-being. By breaking free from the debt trap, you can create a future filled with more choices, opportunities, and freedom to focus on what truly matters.

And because OT student loan debt is likely the primary thing holding you back, in the next chapter we'll do a deep dive into how you pay off your OT student loans quickly.

CHAPTER SEVEN

PAYING OFF YOUR OT STUDENT LOANS QUICKLY: A STEP-BY-STEP GUIDE

"The only way to truly escape the crushing weight of debt is to prioritize freedom over convenience and short-term satisfaction."

– Anonymous

I don't know anyone who would give their 16-year-old, who is still learning to drive, the keys to a Ferrari. There would be about 30 seconds of excitement before the inevitable crash. We'd step back and say: "What was that parent thinking. . .?"

Well, the same is true of universities who saddle undergraduates and graduate students with tens of thousands of student loan debt. Many OTs come out of graduate school with a combined student loan debt of more than $100,000. If you went to a private school, then you could easily owe more than $200,000!

Heck—at least the 16-year-old got some driver's education!

That's in stark contrast to the 18-year-old, or 23-year-old, who have loan documents shoved under their nose and have never taken a personal finance class. Understanding student loans is like learning a foreign language. Subsidized, unsubsidized, ICR, IDR, PAYE, SAVE, PFSL—the acronyms all sound like diagnoses rather than loan terms.

"Doctor, we've got a critical case of unsubsidized ICR in room 3, showing severe symptoms of acute PAYE deficiency. The patient's SAVE levels are off the charts, and their PFSL readings are dangerously low. I recommend an immediate infusion of subsidized terms and a strict regimen of financial counseling. If we don't act fast, we might have to escalate to emergency debt restructuring!"

If you are confused and uncertain about what it all means and how to manage your student loans, then I don't blame you! Let's dive into demystifying all these terms and get you on the road to managing your OT student loans so you can pay them off more quickly.

Subsidized Versus Unsubsidized Loans

On your loan statements you'll probably see that some say "subsidized" while others say "unsubsidized" (or nothing at all). These terms specify whether the loans were accruing interest when you were in school.

Let's take a simple example. Let's say you take out a $30,000 loan to cover tuition for the year at a 6% interest rate. Well, each year this loan generates $1,800 (6% x $30,000) of interest.

If the loan is subsidized, then the federal government "pays" this interest for you. If the loan is unsubsidized, then this $1,800 interest (which you aren't expected to pay since you are in school) is added to the principal balance. So, now you no longer owe $30,000 but instead $31,800.

The distinction between subsidized and unsubsidized only matters while you are in school. After graduation (and any grace period for repayment), these loans are equivalent.

Here are some more details:

- *Subsidized Loans (Federal)*
    - Available only to undergraduate students with demonstrated financial need.
    - The U.S. Department of Education pays the interest on these loans while the student is in school at least half-time, during the grace period after the student leaves school, and during any deferment periods.
    - Helps to reduce the amount of interest that accumulates while the student is not making payments.

- *Unsubsidized Loans (Federal)*
  - Available to undergraduate, graduate, and professional students; no requirement to demonstrate financial need.
  - The borrower is responsible for paying the interest during all periods, including while in school and during grace and deferment periods.
  - Interest accumulates from the time the loan is disbursed.
- *Unsubsidized Loans (Private)*
  - Offered by banks, credit unions, and other private lenders to both undergraduate and graduate students.
  - All private loans are unsubsidized; interest accrues from the time the loan is disbursed.
  - Terms, including interest rates and repayment options, vary by lender and are often based on the borrower's creditworthiness and other factors.

So, what does this mean for the average OT?

- Your federal loans from OT school were unsubsidized (accruing interest during school).
- Your private loans from OT school were also unsubsidized (accruing interest during school).

- Only your federal undergrad loans that were awarded due to financial need were subsidized (not accruing interest during school).

Now, as I mentioned, once you graduate these distinctions are meaningless—you are now in your repayment period, so the loans all behave the same, with you being responsible for the interest. However, it is important to know these terms as you'll see them on your loan statements, and it's easy to get confused.

Much more important is understanding the distinction between private and federal loans and how these differences affect how you should manage your student loan repayments.

Let's dive in.

Private Loans Versus Federal Loans

I'm going to cover the specifics of private loans and federal loans. But first, let's do a high-level comparison of the two to make it simple to refer back to through this chapter and the rest of the book.

Feature	Federal Loans	Private Loans
Eligibility	Based on financial need (for subsidized loans) or enrollment in an eligible program; do not typically require credit checks.	Often based on creditworthiness; may require a co-signer if the borrower has limited or poor credit history.
Interest Rates	Fixed rates set by the government; rates are the same for all borrowers who qualify.	Variable or fixed rates, which can vary based on credit history and lender terms.
Subsidization	Subsidized loans available for undergraduates with financial need (interest paid by government while in school and during grace/deferment periods).	No subsidized options; borrower is responsible for all interest.

Feature	Federal Loans	Private Loans
Repayment Plans	Multiple repayment plans available, including income-driven repayment plans.	Varies by lender; fewer options than federal loans, and typically not based on income.
Forgiveness Programs	Loan forgiveness available for qualifying public service work or under certain income-driven repayment plans.	Rarely offered; terms, if available, vary significantly by lender.
Deferment/ Forbearance	Deferment and forbearance options available for borrowers facing financial hardship.	May be available, but often less flexible than federal loan options.

Feature	Federal Loans	Private Loans
Eligibility for Payoff Programs	Eligible for employer and state payoff programs, which may offer repayment assistance. Specifics depend on the program's criteria.	Also eligible for employer and state payoff programs. The availability and terms of assistance can vary, similar to federal loans.
Refinancing and Consolidation	Federal consolidation available through Direct Loan Consolidation Program, allowing borrowers to combine multiple federal loans into one. Refinancing available through private lenders, potentially at lower interest rates, but may result in loss of federal benefits.	Private loans can be refinanced, often with the goal of securing a lower interest rate. Consolidation of private loans is typically done through refinancing into a new loan.

Unraveling the Mystery of Private Loans: Your Key to Informed Borrowing

Private loans are by far the simplest to understand. These loans are made by banks and other lenders. Private loans aren't eligible for any federal programs for reducing your monthly payments.

Most people max out their federal student loans before taking out private loans, so if you have significant private loans, it typically means that you also have high federal loans and are facing a high overall student loan debt burden.

Since they are private, your ability to "manage" your private loans is limited to (a) refinancing to get lower interest rates and (b) simply paying them off faster. A combination of the two is usually preferable.

It is common to have private student loans with interest rates of 6% to 12% (depending on your credit score and typical interest rates at that time). If you pay off these loans early, you get an immediate return of 6% to 12%. As we talked about in other chapters, choose between an avalanche or snowball method to pay off your student loans early.

Decoding Federal Loans: Navigating the Alphabet Soup of Repayment Options

Federal loans are much more complicated in comparison to private loans. At their core, federal loans operate the same as private loans. You have a principal balance, an interest rate, the length of your loan, and a monthly payment. So far, so good—and the same as private loans.

However, federal loans offer many programs that you can enroll in to:

- Lower your monthly payment below the "full" payment amount
- Forgive your remaining loan balance after certain conditions are met

These programs are filled with acronyms and mystery. Let's peel back the layers.

Slash Your Monthly Payments with These Game-Changing Federal Programs

If you have federal loans, there are multiple programs out there to reduce your monthly payments. These programs change frequently, so it is always worth researching any new program or changes in terms and conditions.

These federal programs all operate in fundamentally the same way:

- Your monthly payment amount is based upon your discretionary income—not your loan balance.
- After you make qualified payments for a certain number of years (typically between 20 and 25 years), the

remaining loan balance is forgiven. However, you have to pay taxes on the amount of loan balance forgiven.

Below is a table of federal programs at the time of publishing.

(See page 153)

As I mentioned, these Income Driven Repayment (IDR) plans change frequently. The ICR plan is the oldest and the SAVE plan is the newest (SAVE replaced REPAYE). What these plans have in common is this concept of "discretionary" income.

What exactly is "discretionary income"? Glad you asked. Discretionary income is based upon the federal poverty levels. The federal poverty levels are in turn based upon family size. In turn, your "discretionary income" is a fixed calculation (not based upon your actual lifestyle costs) and is simply the difference between your income and 150% of the federal poverty level.

To make this concrete, let's use the most popular plan, the SAVE plan, as an example.

Let's say that Amy is an OT and has $100,000 of federal student loan debt with a 6% interest rate and a repayment period of 10 years. Under those terms, her monthly payment should be $1,110.21.

Under SAVE, we look at her family size and their household income to determine what her monthly payment will be.

Plan Name	Calculation Method	Eligibility	Accrued Interest Treatment	Loan Balance Forgiveness
Saving on a Valuable Education (SAVE) Plan	10% of discretionary income (dropping to 5% for undergraduate loans in July 2024).	Direct Loans (both undergraduate and graduate students).	100% of unpaid interest is covered by the government—your loan balance will never increase due to unpaid interest.	20 years for undergraduate loans; 25 years for graduate loans. Loans under $12,000 are forgiven after 10 years.
Pay As You Earn (PAYE)	10% of your discretionary income, but never more than the 10-year Standard Repayment Plan amount.	Must be a new borrower on or after Oct. 1, 2007, and must have received a disbursement of a Direct Loan on or after	The government pays the unpaid interest on subsidized loans for the first three years. After that, interest capitalizes if	After 20 years.

Income-Based Repayment (IBR)	10% (new borrowers on/after July 1, 2014) or 15% (others) of your discretionary income, but never more than the 10-year Standard Repayment Plan amount.	Oct. 1, 2011. Direct Loans only. For Direct and FFEL Loans. New borrower requirement for 10% calculation.	not paid by the borrower. The government pays the unpaid interest on subsidized loans for the first three years. After that, interest capitalizes if not paid by the borrower.	After 20 years for new borrowers on/after July 1, 2014; 25 years for others.
Income-Contingent Repayment (ICR)	The lesser of 20% of your discretionary income or what you would pay on a repayment plan with a fixed payment over 12 years, adjusted according to your income.	Direct Loans only; available to borrowers with Parent PLUS loans if they are consolidated into a Direct Consolidation Loan.	Interest capitalizes if not paid by the borrower. There is no subsidy benefit like there is in SAVE, PAYE, or IBR.	After 25 years.

Let's say she is single (family size = 1) and has a household income of $70,000.

We will assume that all the loans are graduate loans so the 10% discretionary income calculation applies. If the borrower had undergraduate loans, their payment percentage would decrease to 5% starting in July 2024.

Here's how the calculations would break down:

Description	Calculation/Amount
Annual Income	$70,000
Family Size	1
Federal Poverty Guideline (FPG) for Family Size	$13,590
150% of FPG	$20,385 (= $13,590 x 1.5)
Discretionary Income	$49,615 (= $70,000 - $20,385)
Percentage of Discretionary Income to be Paid	10%
Annual SAVE Payment	$4,961.50 (= 10% of $49,615)
Monthly SAVE Payment	$413.46 (= $4,961.50/12)

Under SAVE, Amy would only have to pay $413.46/month on her federal loans. That's a big reduction from her standard payment of $1,110.21 (decreasing by close to $700/month!).

Now, let's consider a scenario of Sarah, an OT who is married with two kids and has a gross taxable household income of $150,000 combined with her spouse. Here is how the calculation works for this

Description	Calculation/Amount
Annual Income	$150,000
Family Size	4
Federal Poverty Guideline (FPG) for Family Size	$27,750
150% of FPG	$41,625 (= $27,750 x 1.5)
Discretionary Income	$108,375 (= $150,000 - $41,625)
Percentage of Discretionary Income to be Paid	10%
Annual SAVE Payment	$10,837.50 (= 10% of $108,375)
Monthly SAVE Payment	$903.13 (= $10,837.50 / 12)

In this example, the monthly SAVE loan amount would be $903.13/month instead of the original amount of $1,110.21. You can see the impact making more money makes on the overall SAVE amount. In fact, because the SAVE amount is based only on your household income (and not your loan amount) you can get to a point where your SAVE amount is above your standard repayment amount!

Of course, reducing your monthly payment helps you manage your monthly expenses and create some breathing room in your monthly budget. However, if you suspect there must be a "catch" for reducing your monthly payments, you are 100% correct. It is important to understand and consider the entirety of IDR plans rather than only focusing on the monthly reduction in your payments. Understanding the pros and cons will enable you to understand better the cost of your decisions.

SAVE: The Insider's Guide to the Pros, Cons, and Everything in Between

Let's focus on the most popular IDR plan, the SAVE program. The Department of Education has replaced REPAYE with SAVE, making significant improvements to the program. While government action doesn't happen overnight, many of the other older programs aren't as popular. Given this potential and the popularity of SAVE, it is especially important to understand this program.

It is obvious from the previous section that the major pro is that SAVE can reduce (sometimes significantly) the amount you need to pay each month. Couple that with a loan forgiveness after 25 years, and this seems like a *slam dunk*!

Not so fast. Like yin and yang, there is a major con that comes with this and that is rarely discussed. After 25 years, any remaining loan balance that is forgiven is treated as *taxable income* for that year - depending upon future tax laws.

For example, if you end up with $90,000 of loan balance that is forgiven, then the IRS will treat this as "income" for that calendar year. You'll have to pay taxes on this $90,000 forgiven amount. Depending upon your overall income level, your state, etc., you could easily end up owing the IRS $25,000 to $30,000 in taxes.

Most people aren't aware of this or, if they are, they aren't saving up right now for this tax bill.

It can lead to some nasty surprises.

However, SAVE fixed a big issue that was present under the original REPAYE program. Under the REPAYE program your loan balance could actually grow over time due to unpaid interest accumulation.

But, here's the big update with SAVE:

- Your loan balance will no longer increase due to unpaid interest. Under REPAYE, if your monthly payment didn't cover the full interest charge, the unpaid portion was added to your loan balance - causing it to grow instead of shrink

- SAVE eliminates this problem. The government now covers 100% of unpaid interest, ensuring that your loan balance never increases due to interest accumulation.

This is one of the biggest changes that makes SAVE far more borrower-friendly than REPAYE.

Under SAVE, your loan can end up costing you more than under a standard repayment plan. And that is due to a combination of two things: the longer repayment period and the potential tax-bomb at the end.

Let's look at the example of Amy to make this easy to understand.

- She has a $100,000 loan at 6% interest. That means that every year, she should be paying $6,000 in interest (not principal) payments. That is $500/month.
- She has a SAVE amount of $413.46/month.
- Under REPAYE, this would have been a problem. Since her payment is lower than her interest charge, the loan balance would have grown with unpaid interest.
- Under SAVE, this problem is gone. The government covers 100% of the unpaid interest, so her loan balance never increases.

- However, since her payments don't even cover the full interest charge, none of her monthly payments will be applied towards her principal loan balance of $100k.

- This means that after 25 years, the amount that will be forgiven is $100k as she didn't pay down any principal.

- She will owe taxes on the $100k that gets forgiven according to future tax laws. If she is in a 25% tax bracket this would result in a $25k tax bill.

In the words of infomercials everywhere... That's not all! She has been making her monthly payment of $413.46/month for 25 years. That means her monthly payments have totaled $124,038. So the total cost to Amy of doing SAVE is $149,038!

If she had stayed with her original terms, the total cost of her loan would have only been $133,200. She has paid over $15,000 extra under SAVE. Of course, her monthly payments have been much lower, which may be what is required from a cashflow perspective.

I like this example because it shines light on the rarely discussed implications of programs like SAVE.

To recap Amy's situation:

Repayment Plan	Years	Monthly Payment	Total of Monthly Payments	Total Tax Liability (estimated)	Total Cost of Loan	Notes
Standard Repayment	10	$1,110	$133,200	N/A	$133,200	Payments stop after 10 years.
SAVE	25	$414	$124,038	$25,000	$149,038	Payments are lower but extend for 25 years. Tax liability on forgiven amount.

Of course, if you have a higher income, then your monthly payment will be higher. And in that case, you may be paying off a part of the principal of the loan each month. As your income increases, the amount you pay under SAVE increases and you can end up paying as much or more (there is no cap) than your standard repayment.

The SAVE program is great for lowering your monthly payments, but *it doesn't help you get out of debt*. That's a huge and important distinction, since getting out of debt quickly is the top priority to focus on to build financial freedom.

To summarize, here are the pros and cons of the SAVE program:

Pros of SAVE	Cons of SAVE
Payments based on income, which can lower your monthly payments	May pay more over time
Lower payments for undergraduates (5% instead of 10%)	Parent PLUS loans still not eligible
Interest subsidy prevents balance growth	No cap on payments for high earners
Loan forgiveness after 20/25 years depending upon undergrad/graduate loans	Annual income recertification required
No income eligibility requirement	Possible tax on forgiven amount

When I talk with OTs about the pros and cons of SAVE and other IDR programs, they are usually surprised about the potential tax bomb at the end. That is because they are usually thinking about a specific program called Public Service Loan Forgiveness (PSLF).

PSLF: Is This Loan Forgiveness Program Right for You?

The Public Service Loan Forgiveness (PSLF) program has specific requirements. Before getting into the specifics, let's clear the air a little bit and make sure we have our terminology straight:

The IDR plans (e.g. SAVE, etc.) that we just discussed are open to anyone with federal loans.

Remember that potential tax bomb we talked about in the last section? That doesn't happen under PSLF. After 10 years of qualified payments, the remaining balance of your loan is forgiven, and you don't pay taxes on it.

Here is the flow:

- You enroll in an IDR plan to reduce your monthly payments.
- You then enroll in PSLF to have your balance forgiven (tax free) after 120 qualifying payments.

Many people discuss IDR, PSLF, and other programs interchangeably, but this isn't correct. While anyone with federal loans can qualify for an IDR plan, not everyone will qualify for PSLF. So, let's look at the requirements for PSLF. To qualify for PSLF you must:

Requirement	Description
Employment	Work full-time for a qualifying employer (government organizations, non-profits, etc.).
Loan Type	Have Direct Federal Loans or consolidate other federal student loans into a Direct Loan.
Repayment Plan	Be enrolled in an Income-Driven Repayment (IDR) plan.
Qualifying Payments	Make 120 qualifying payments (payments made under the IDR plan while working for a qualifying employer).
Certification	Submit the Employment Certification Form annually or when changing employers to track qualifying employment and payments.

There are a few components here of which you need to be aware:

- It has to be a qualifying employer—not just any employer
- You have to make 120 one-time monthly payments (10 years)
- For your monthly payment to qualify you must be working more than 30 hours a week
- You must be an employee of the company—1099 contractors don't qualify
- You must be detailed, keeping records of all your qualifying payments, your employment certification form, etc.

The PSLF can be a great triple-whammy because you get a lower monthly payment (under the IDR plans), you stop paying after 10 years (compared to 25 years under IDR), and the loan balance at 10 years is forgiven without a tax bill (unlike non-PSLF under IDR).

Let's take another look at the example of Amy from the last section. Remember her? She was the one who had the big tax bill coming. She ended up paying much more for the loan under SAVE than if she just paid under the standard repayment plan.

Well, after signing up to SAVE (reducing her payment to $414/month), working for a qualifying employer, and following all the stipulations outlined to be eligible for PSLF, after 10 years (120 payments), she will have paid a total of $49,680. At that point, she can stop her monthly payments and have the rest of her loan balance ($100,000) forgiven tax-free.

So, in this example, here is the comparison between three choices she had:

1. Stick with the original repayment plan: $1,110/month for 10 years. Total loan would cost $133,200.
2. Do SAVE only: $414/month for 25 years. Total loan (with the tax bill) would cost $149,038.
3. Do SAVE with PSLF: $414 for 10 years. Total loan (with no tax bill) would cost $49,680.

Comparing these, PSLF is the clear winner in terms of (a) monthly payments and (b) total amount.

Now, as Amy's income grows, she will have to increase her monthly payments, and so her total loan cost would go up.

Numbers don't always tell the full human story, and that's where we need to consider a few things. Let's put ourselves in Amy's shoes for a moment and imagine a few scenarios:

- What if she starts a family (or already has a family) and wants to reduce her hours to 25 per week? Sorry, she must work 30 hours or more each week for her payments to qualify.

- What if she wants to become a 1099 contractor to earn more money as an OT? Sorry, only W2 employees qualify.

- What if she sees a job posting at a local clinic paying $15k more than she's making now? Oops, sorry, that clinic isn't a qualifying employer, and if you move for a higher salary then you lose PSLF. In ten years she'd earn at least an extra $150k at this higher paying job. This could make losing PSLF worth it, potentially. But many don't run the numbers and stay with PSLF even when it doesn't make long-term financial sense.

- What if she discovers a specialty within OT that she wants to now work in? If she can't find that at a qualifying employer in town then she must make a hard decision. Pursue her passion (what makes her happy) or keep on the PSLF.

It is hard to predict the next 10 years of anything, let alone your passions, your family situation, other life events, etc.

While PSLF can reduce your overall debt burden, it comes with a trade-off. And that trade-off is that essentially for 10 years you'll have a second (or maybe third!) boss called PSLF that you need to run every decision by. Depending upon your situation, it can quickly start to feel like your entire life revolves around PSLF. It can start to feel like a golden cage or golden handcuffs.

That doesn't mean it doesn't have its place, and isn't right in some situations, but I want you to be fully aware of the trade-offs.

To summarize, here are the pros and cons of PSLF.

Pros of PSLF	Cons of PSLF
Loan Forgiveness: Remaining balance forgiven after 120 qualifying payments.	**Full-Time Requirement**: Must work full-time, potentially interfering with life events/plans.
Tax-Free Forgiveness: Forgiven amount is not taxable income.	**Employment Restrictions**: Limited ability to increase salary due to qualifying employment requirements.
Supports Public Service: Encourages work in nonprofit and government sectors.	**Complex Eligibility**: Specific requirements for qualifying payments and employment can be complex.
Use with IDR Plans: Lowers monthly payments before forgiveness.	**Documentation**: Requires diligent record-keeping and annual submission of employment certification.

What's the Deal with Consolidation and Refinancing?

These are two words that are thrown around a lot, so let's discuss them quickly before we talk about strategies to pay off your student loans faster.

Consolidation

Consolidation typically occurs with federal loans and involves combining all your individual loans into one loan. This doesn't lower your interest rate or your monthly payments, and the new interest rate is the weighted average of the individual loans that were consolidated. Some federal programs require consolidation.

Refinancing

Refinancing is typically done with private lenders and used to change the interest rate (and term) of the loans. Unlike consolidation, refinancing can significantly alter the interest rate based on the borrower's creditworthiness and market conditions.

Refinancing can be a great option if you have private loans. You should refinance when rates are lower, since a lower interest rate typically means lower monthly payments and a lower total cost of your loans. You can do this as often as you want, though be aware that there may be other fees for refinancing.

However, you must be careful. Do not refinance federal loans into private loans if you plan on doing any IDR or PSLF program. When you refinance a federal loan into a private lender, then those loans are no longer eligible for IDR or PFLF due to no longer being classified as federal loans.

Accelerate Your Journey to Debt Freedom: Proven Tactics to Pay Off Your Loans Faster

The entire purpose of this book is to get you on the path to being financially free. To experience financial abundance. To experience financial freedom. To have a choice in your life in how you spend your time, who you spend it with, and how you get to live. I want you to have freedom—I think you and everyone else deserve it.

After all, despite our best intentions, if we repeatedly *have to* do something, even something we enjoy, it can quickly feel unpleasant. And the calculus of becoming financially free is simple:

1. Reduce our monthly expenses
2. Increase our monthly income
3. Save and invest the difference over a long time

The longer we stretch out our monthly payments, the longer it takes us to start investing and building wealth.

So here is my advice:

- Enrolling in an IDR plan is great to reduce your monthly expenses and frees you up to have a bit of breathing room. But don't plan on being on an IDR forever.
- Instead, start making extra payments to pay off your student loans faster—there is no prepayment penalty.

In Chapter 6, we covered the two different approaches to paying down debt: the avalanche method and the snowball method. Those are the two big categories of debt paydown, but there are additional strategies that you can apply in each.

Strategy 1: Sign up for autopay. Many lenders will give you a discount of 0.25% to 0.5% off the interest rate if you sign up for automatic payments. If you have a $100,000 loan with 10 years at 6%, your monthly payment would be about $1,120/month with a total cost of $133,225. If you get a 0.5% reduction then you'd pay $1,085/month with a total cost of $130,242, saving you about $3k for about an hour of work to enroll in autopay.

Strategy 2: Any time you refinance your private loans, if possible, keep paying the old (higher) amount, as you've already gotten used to paying that amount. This higher amount will pay down your principal faster, resulting in paying less overall interest and paying off your loan faster. Taking the previous example, if you pay $1,120/month instead of $1,085, then you'll pay off the loan in 9 years and 1 month and save about $10k in the process. If you refinanced from 7% to 5% and maintained the higher monthly payments, then you could pay off your loan in 8.75 years and save $19k in interest.

Strategy 3: Make biweekly payments. Instead of making one monthly payment, you divide your monthly payment by two and make the payment every two weeks. This is a sneaky strategy because this actually means you are making 26 biweekly payments, which is equivalent to 13 monthly payments. It is like making one extra payment a year. The impact can be huge, because every two weeks you are paying off a little bit of principal. The more regularly you pay off your principal, the faster you pay off the loan. Take a look at the below table:

Loan Terms: 10-Year, $100,000 at 6% Interest	Standard Monthly Payment: $1,120	Biweekly Payment: $560
Year #	Standard Principal Remaining	Biweekly Principal Remaining
1	$92,472.78	$91,299.26
2	$84,481.29	$82,063.03
3	$75,996.91	$72,258.35
4	$66,989.23	$61,850.24
5	$57,425.98	$50,801.55
6	$47,272.88	$39,072.86
7	$36,493.57	$26,622.32
8	$25,049.41	$13,405.51
9	$12,899.40	$0.00
10	$0.00	$0.00

Under biweekly payments, the loan gets paid off in under nine years with huge savings in interest, just from a simple switch.

Strategy 4: Anytime you get extra money, put it toward your loan. Let's say you get an unexpected tax refund of $2,800. Put it right toward your loans. Sell something? Put it right toward your loans. Get a raise of a few hundred a month? Put it right toward your loans. Remember, any extra money you can put toward the principal will allow you to pay off your loans faster *and* save money by not paying so much in interest.

Strategy 5: All the above strategies are great, and you should start doing them immediately. In doing so, you won't notice much difference in your daily or monthly life, because we've automated some things and changed how and when we pay extra. While these will reduce the overall cost of your loans, you'll still end up paying on the loans for a long time.

What we need to do is start paying *a lot* extra on your loans each month. Remember, the goal is to be debt-free in no longer than three years. This is 100% doable but requires that we come up with extra money to throw at your student loans.

To accomplish this, depending upon your loan balance, it would be ideal to be paying an extra $2k to $3k per month toward your student loans.

And we need to do this through a combination of strategies:

1. Reduce your monthly expenses and send the extra money toward your student loans.
2. Increase your monthly income and send the extra money toward your student loans.

Ideally, we can use a combination of the two strategies above.

Let's take a concrete example so you can see how this all works out. Let's say you have $100,000 of student loan debt with a 10-year repayment period and 7% interest rate. As we've covered before, your monthly payment will be about $1,161.

If we set a goal of paying off our student loan in three years, then we need to pay about $3,000/month toward our student loans. This means we need to pay about an extra $1,900/month.

So, we ask a curiosity question: How do we get an extra $1,900/month to pay toward our student loans? In other words: "How do we decrease our monthly expenses and increase our monthly income so that we have an extra $1,900/month?"

Well, here are some potential ways:

1. If you just graduated, then perhaps you live with your parents for the first couple years. This would free up a lot of money each month.
2. You delay living alone and split your rent with friends.
3. You move into a lower cost of living place.
4. You sell the car with expensive monthly payments and replace it with a beater for a third of the cost.
5. You reduce your entertainment and food expenses.
6. You take on a per diem job for a few hours a week to earn extra income.
7. You start seeing clients on the side and charge cash—this is my favorite way for increasing your income, and we cover this in Chapter 9.

You could come up with a ton of ideas. To keep this example going, let's say you go through everything and do the following:

1. You scrub your monthly budget to come up with an extra $1,000/month.
2. You start seeing clients privately and on the side. You charge $125/session (this is on the low end). After accounting for taxes, you need to see only nine private clients a month to earn an extra $900. So, you set up your little side practice seeing clients part-time and average two to three clients a week.

Between these two strategies, you'll have an extra $1,900/month to pay toward your student loans and will be student loan free in three years. And the great thing is that after those three years, you'll be used to making $3,000/month payments, which you can then put toward investing moving forward.

Now, your loan situation is obviously different. But this is the throughline that you need to follow to pay off your loans faster.

Does it require sacrifice and getting creative? Absolutely. Is it a walk in the park? No, it requires you to forgo some things in the short term. You know what also requires sacrifice? Being controlled for *decades* by your student loan debt. So, we can either sacrifice in the short term or sacrifice in the long term. Remember, the sacrifice will end, but the results will last.

I've never met an OT who regrets paying off their student loan debt early and aggressively. They are usually the ones who have a little more bounce in their step and a lot less pressure in their life and are on the path of being able to focus their efforts on what brings them the most joy.

With this newfound freedom, you'll have even more money to invest and reach financial freedom.

CHAPTER EIGHT

INVESTING 101: WHAT EVERY OT SEEKING FINANCIAL FREEDOM SHOULD KNOW

"Every dollar you invest is a seed; the sooner you plant, the larger your forest will grow."

– Unknown

Investing your money tends to bring up a lot of confusion. There is a ton of jargon, acronyms, and just plain mystery around investing that is enough to stop a lot of people in their tracks.

In this chapter, we will cover the following concepts and information:

- Overview of asset classes
- Overview of investment accounts
- Top myths about investing

- What the wealthy know about investing
- How to start investing your money

Mainstream media often seems to make investing as confusing as possible. But after this chapter, you are going to know more than 99% of the population when it comes to investing, including what to avoid and how to put investing on autopilot so you don't need to think about it.

The two biggest areas of confusion I see in the media and my clients are usually around assets and accounts. This confusion looks like the following exchange:

"What are you invested in?"

"Oh, I invest in my 401k."

"Okay, well, your 401k is just an account. Inside your 401k, what have you invested in?"

"Oh, I just know it is a 401k..."

It might seem nitpicky, but it is important to understand the difference between assets and accounts. Put simply, assets are *what* you invest in, and accounts are *where* your assets are housed. Let's break down the most common assets and the most common accounts so that you understand the difference and know what to prioritize.

Mastering the Building Blocks of Investing: Assets and Accounts

Overview of Asset Classes

If we had to generalize as to why some people achieve financial freedom and some people don't, we might say: "People with financial freedom focus on purchasing things that increase in value, while others purchase things that decrease in value."

Stocks

Stocks represent a share of ownership in a company. When you buy a stock, you're essentially buying a tiny piece of that company. The value of your stock goes up or down based on how well the company is doing and how investors believe the company will perform in the future. Think of it as having a small stake in a large pie—the better the pie (the company) does, the more your slice is worth. You can buy single stocks or baskets of stocks.

Bonds

Bonds can be thought of as a loan you give to a government or a corporation, and in return, they promise to pay you back the principal amount plus interest, in the future. The interest is usually paid at regular intervals (annually, semi-annually, etc.). Bonds are considered less risky than stocks because you're supposed to get your money back plus interest, making them a good choice for those who want a steadier, more predictable income. However, compared to stocks, the average returns are smaller.

Commodities

Commodities include physical goods like gold, oil, and agricultural products. Investing in commodities can mean directly buying physical goods, investing in commodity futures contracts, or investing in commodity-related stocks. Prices for commodities can be volatile, influenced by factors like weather, political instability, and changes in supply and demand. Due to this volatility and complexity, commodities aren't ideal for newbie investors.

Real Estate

Real estate investing involves buying property to generate income or to sell at a profit. This can include residential properties, commercial properties, or land. Real estate can provide a steady income through rentals and potential tax advantages. You can invest in real estate by physically purchasing the real estate (e.g. you buy a duplex in your hometown and rent it out). Alternatively, there are publicly traded shares of real estate portfolio companies that you can buy and sell like stocks.

Invariably someone will look at the above list and shout at me: "What about Bitcoin?" or "What about investing in wine?" or "What about my investments in rare Pokémon cards?"

Well, I'm not going to cover those alternative asset classes, because they are much more esoteric, typically illiquid (not cash or easily convertible to cash), require a high degree of risk tolerance, and aren't something you should worry about when you are beginning to invest.

In fact, the vast majority of people should focus on two asset classes, particularly when just starting to invest:

1. Stocks
2. Bonds

Now, there is all sorts of advice out there regarding what percentage of stocks you should have versus the percentage of bonds. You'll hear conflicting things like:

- 100 minus your age is the percentage you should have in stocks
- Or, more recently, 120 minus your age is the percentage you should have in stocks due to the increase in life expectancy
- Do a 60/40 portfolio
- And so on...

My advice to you is: unless you are sophisticated, it is a good idea to just purchase a Target Date fund that will automatically invest in a mix of stocks and bonds for you and adjust the ratio of stocks and bonds as you get closer to your "retirement date."

It takes the guesswork out of figuring out the percentages and having to rebalance the portfolio itself. Plus, you can purchase target date funds that invest in thousands of companies so you get diversification.

Companies like Vanguard offer the ability to start investing in target date funds with a minimum balance of only $1,000. And Vanguard is the industry leader in terms of offering low-cost investments, so you keep more of your returns versus paying the company.

Navigating the Investment Account Maze: Your Key to Financial Success

Overview of Investment Accounts

The asset classes you are investing in are incredibly important (in terms of the returns/risk, etc.), but the actual account itself where you are doing the investing is equally important.

Not all investment accounts are created equal. There is a never-ending and confusing array of investment accounts with different benefits and features, which makes it important to understand them and the differences between them.

Navigating various investment accounts is crucial for achieving your financial goals. Each account has its own set of rules, tax benefits, and, in some cases, contribution limits. Because of this, there is actually a preferred optimal "order" in which to invest. I'll explain as we go.

First, here are the different investment accounts we will be discussing:

- 401(k)
- 403(b)
- Traditional IRA
- Roth IRA
- Health Savings Account (HSA)
- Taxable brokerage account

Here's an overview of each:

401(k)

A 401(k) is a retirement savings plan offered by employers that allows employees to save and invest a piece of their paychecks *before* taxes are taken out. Contributions reduce taxable income, and earnings grow tax deferred, meaning that you do not pay taxes until the money is distributed in retirement. Many employers match contributions to some extent, such as up to 3% or 5%, enhancing the value of this account. For those under 50, the annual contribution limit is $23,500 as of 2025. Individuals 50 and older can contribute an additional $7,500 as a catch-up, totaling $31,000.

403(b)

The 403(b) plan is similar to the 401(k) but is available to employees of tax-exempt organizations. It allows pre-tax contributions, tax-deferred growth, and sometimes employer matching. The contribution limits are identical to those of the 401(k) plans, fostering retirement savings among teachers, nonprofit workers, and hospital employees.

Traditional IRA

A Traditional IRA offers the ability to make pre-tax contributions, potentially reducing your taxable income for the year of contribution. The investment growth is tax-deferred, so taxes are paid upon withdrawal in retirement. The 2025 contribution limit is $7,000 for those under 50, with a $1,000 catch-up contribution for those 50 and older, making it $8,000 in total.

Roth IRA

Contributions to a Roth IRA are made with after-tax money, meaning withdrawals in retirement are tax-free, provided certain conditions are met. This makes the Roth

IRA a powerful tool for tax-free income in retirement. The contribution limits are the same as the Traditional IRA. However, Roth IRAs have income limits for eligibility.[7]

Health Savings Account (HSA)

An HSA is available to those with high-deductible health plans and offers triple tax advantages: contributions reduce taxable income, earnings grow tax-free, and withdrawals for qualified medical expenses are tax-free. For 2025, the contribution limit is $4,300 for individual coverage and $8,550 for family coverage, with an additional $1,000 allowed for those 55 and older.

Taxable Brokerage Account

A taxable brokerage account doesn't offer specific tax advantages for contributions or earnings, and there are no contribution limits. It offers the flexibility to invest in stocks, bonds, mutual funds, and other securities. Capital gains are taxed in the year in which they are realized (e.g. the year you sell) while dividends are taxed in the year in which

---

[7] Contribution limits and eligibility normally change year to year. The best way to find the current limits and eligibility is to Google "IRS contribution limits (insert year) for (insert type of account)." So, for instance you'd Google "IRS contribution limits 2026 for Roth IRA."

they were received. This account type is valuable for goals outside of retirement or for when you've already maxed out tax-advantaged accounts, since it has no contribution limits or penalties on withdrawals.

Contribution Limits Note[8]:

You'll see that I reference contribution limits to 401(k)'s, Roth IRAs, etc. throughout the book and in examples. This book was originally published in 2025 so these amounts reflect what is allowed in that year. However, each year the contribution limits normally change due to inflation and other economic variables. Don't worry, the concepts are still exactly the same even if the amounts change slightly from year to year. To find the most up to date contribution limits after 2025 I recommend you Google the phrase "IRS contribution limits (type of account) in (year)." So, for instance you'd Google "IRS contribution limits Roth IRA in 2027."

---

8 *401(k)/403(b): $23,500 under 50, $31,000 age 50+ (catch-up contribution).

**Traditional/Roth IRA: $7,000 under 50, $8,000 age 50+ (catch-up contribution).

***HSA: $4,300 for individual coverage, $8,550 for family coverage, plus $1,000 catch-up for those 55+.

Below is a table summarizing all the different features and benefits of the different account types. At first glance, this table is going to seem overwhelming. . . but don't worry, these concepts will be easy to understand. If you've made it through OT grad school, then you can understand this.

Attribute	401(k)	403(b)
Contributions Pre-Tax	✓	✓
Growth Tax-Deferred	✓	✓
Distributions Tax-Free	✗	✗
Contributions After-Tax	✗	✗
Employer Match Available	✓	✓
Penalty-Free Withdrawal Before Age 59.5	✗	✗
Contribution Limits	$23,500/$31,000*	$23,500/$31,000*
Income Limits for Eligibility	✗	✗
Investment Options	Wide range	Wide range
Tax Advantages	Pre-tax contributions; tax-deferred growth	Pre-tax contributions; tax-deferred growth

Attribute	Traditional IRA	Roth IRA
Contributions Pre-Tax	✓	✗
Growth Tax-Deferred	✓	✓
Distributions Tax-Free	✗	✓
Contributions After-Tax	✗	✓
Employer Match Available	✗	✗
Penalty-Free Withdrawal Before Age 59.5	Special conditions apply	Special conditions apply
Contribution Limits	$7,000/$8,000**	$7,000/$8,000**
Income Limits for Eligibility	✗	✓
Investment Options	Wide range	Wide range
Tax Advantages	Pre-tax contributions; tax-deferred growth	Tax-free distributions; contributions with after-tax money

Attribute	HSA	Taxable Brokerage
Contributions Pre-Tax	✓	✗
Growth Tax-Deferred	✓	✗
Distributions Tax-Free	For medical expenses	✗
Contributions After-Tax	✗	✓
Employer Match Available	✗	✗
Penalty-Free Withdrawal Before Age 59.5	For medical expenses	✓
Contribution Limits	$4,300/$8,550***	No limit
Income Limits for Eligibility	✗	✗
Investment Options	Limited	Widest range
Tax Advantages	Triple tax advantage: contributions, growth, and distributions for medical expenses	None (capital gains and dividends taxed annually)

There are two key attributes you need to focus on and understand. The first is that a lot of the rows are focused on taxes. How your investments are taxed plays a huge role in determining the order of priority in investing. I'll explain in a later section, but keep in the back of your mind that it is much better to have your investments grow tax-free than to pay taxes all the time.

The second is: you can see how some accounts, the 401(k) and 403(b), allow for an employer match. Definitely take advantage of receiving an employer match, which is usually around 5%. This means that if you contribute 5% your employer will kick in another 5% in "match." This doubles your 5% contribution to 10% immediately. It is "free" money that your employer is giving you as part of your employee benefit—not taking advantage of this is literally giving up free money.

You'll want to refer back to this table through the rest of this chapter as we will be using aspects of it to both debunk myths about investing and provide guidance on how to invest and what order to prioritize and maximize your accounts.

Debunking Investment Myths: Empowering OTs to Take Control

The talking heads on CNBC and other programs will have you believe that investing is incredibly complex, scary, and that you must spend hours upon hours reading boring financial statements to have any luck at all.

On the other side, you have TV shows and movies featuring a rich person who has "inside knowledge" about some particular stock or investment that he shares with his closest friends.

There is so much misinformation out there about investing that it can seem that average people like you and me don't stand a chance. Fortunately, this is all hogwash, and you and I do stand a chance.

However, this requires us to tackle some of the most common myths and misconceptions about investing so that we get crystal clear clarity about what to do and what not to do.

Myth 1: Investing Is Only for the Wealthy

The image of investors sitting in a dark paneled room inside a cloistered country club smoking cigars and drinking whiskey and "buying and selling companies" is something that persists to this day. Given images like this, it is easy to think that investing is only for the wealthy. That there is an "old boys club" and if you aren't a part of it, then tough luck.

Fortunately, this isn't true. You can open a Roth IRA at Vanguard with no minimum balance and start investing immediately. With huge brokerage firms like Vanguard and

Fidelity, there have never been lower barriers in place to start investing right away.

Myth 2: Investing Is Like Gambling

Another myth about investing is that it is akin to gambling. There is a big difference between betting on black in Las Vegas and buying shares of Apple, Amazon, or other companies.

Investing does involve risk. This risk is mitigated through diversifying your investments and having a long-time horizon. Investing isn't about "making a quick buck" but rather taking a long-term view that there will be continuous development by companies, that the economy will continue to grow, and that innovation over decades will lead to an increase in economic output.

Myth 3: Investing Is Risky—It Is Better to Keep Money in Cash

Investing does involve risk. In the short term you may actually lose money, because no one knows if the stock market will go up or down. And so, many people will think to themselves: *I don't want to lose money, so I'll just keep it in cash.*

The big problem with this is that inflation is eating away at your purchasing power over time.

Inflation averages 2 to 3% a year, which means that each year, the cost of items you purchase goes up. This means something that costs $10,000 today will likely cost about $18,000 twenty years in the future.

The only way to combat the erosion in your purchasing power over time is to invest your money and have your money grow at a rate above inflation. That means investing your money, because a surefire way to lose money is not to invest and, instead, let inflation erode your purchasing power.

Myth 4: Investing Is Complicated and Takes Too Much Time

There is a big difference between investing and trading. Trading is what most people think of when they think of investing. Trading looks like reading the WSJ every morning, keeping your eyes peeled to CNBC every hour and monitoring your investment portfolio every minute trying to decide "should I sell?" or "should I buy some more?"

That's not investing. The investing I'm talking about is super boring. It is "buy and hold." It isn't sexy. It isn't dynamic. And it isn't complicated. And it certainly doesn't take up much time.

In fact, you should automate it so that a certain amount of money is being invested each month such that you don't even have to think about it except to review your account statements each month or quarter.

Myth 5: You Need to Be an Expert to Invest

There is no shortage of "experts" out there that will tell you why you need their advice to be successful. And they do a great job making investing overly complicated and making you feel that you are inadequate to invest your own money. After all, how could you know more than someone who does investing and advising full time?

You can buy shares in actively managed funds where there is a fund manager behind the scenes whose sole job is to pick and choose what investments to buy and sell. This person has access to all of the latest research, a plethora of investment analysts working for them, and literally watches the market like a hawk.

Guess what? Studies upon studies show that actively managed funds (e.g. the "experts") underperform year after year compared with a much simpler strategy: just buying low-cost index funds that passively replicate the market. To put it in layman's terms: the experts charge a lot only to underperform the market on average.

The punchline? You don't need to be an expert to invest. You need to focus on low-cost index funds that replicate a benchmark passively. If you do that, you'll outperform 99% of the "experts."

Myth 6: You Can Get Rich Quick Investing

You can hear about someone buying a stock right before a huge announcement. Perhaps they "made three times their money overnight!"

That's not investing. That is speculation. Speculating occurs when you take a view on what a company's stock will do over the short term. And to me, that's gambling, because literally no one knows what is going to happen over the short term.

You can get rich investing (and will), but it will happen slowly. Historically, the average market return in the stock market has been about 10 to 12% a year, depending which time period you are looking at. You won't get rich quickly with 10 to 12% returns—but you will get rich slowly, which is less risky and more sustainable.

Myth 7: Timing the Market is Key to Investing

I'll say it again—absolutely no one knows where the market is headed over the short term. There are millions of investors trading shares every single day.

If someone sells, they do so because they think the market will go down. But... for them to be able to sell their shares, there must be a buyer on the other end of the transaction. And so, the only reason someone will buy is because they think the shares will go up. So in every transaction, you have one person who thinks it will go down and another who thinks it will go up.

Who is right? No one knows in the short term. Over the long term, though, the market tends to go up, which is why there is the investing adage: "Time in the market, rather than timing the market, is key to building wealth."

With the myths covered, let's turn our attention to what the wealthy *do* know about investing.

Unlocking the Secrets of Wealth: Investment Wisdom for OTs

Investing is the key to overcoming the impact of inflation and growing your money so you have assets that will fund your retirement.

So, how do you actually become wealthy from investing? The key is to follow certain principles that have been proven, throughout time, to work.

The Hidden Costs Draining Your Investment Potential

Successful Investing Principle 1: Embrace Cost Awareness

Most investors don't realize how much their returns are impacted by various fees and costs. Your goal as a successful investor is to reduce the amount of fees you pay to the lowest you can. Any fees you pay directly impact your returns and, thus, how much money you'll have in retirement.

Fees crop up in many ways:

- Paying an investment advisor to manage your money
- Transaction fees from actively managed investments
- Management fees on actively managed investments
- Taxes on transactions every time you buy or sell

Let's take a simple example. If you pay an investment advisor to manage your money, they could charge you 1% to manage your money. They will likely put your investments into an actively managed fund where you could end up paying another 1.5%. In addition, because it is an actively managed fund, they are constantly trading, which comes with transaction costs and short-term taxes. That could add another 1 to 2% in costs. All told, you may end up paying 4.5% in costs each year.

I'll put it bluntly—this is highway robbery.

If you invest in passively managed funds through companies like Vanguard or Fidelity, you could pay fees as low as 0.03%. Think about it—paying 0.03% instead of up to 4.5%. This has a huge impact on the overall growth of your money.

Let's say you have $10,000 to invest with an annual return of 10%. Well, after 20 years:

- The actively managed portfolio with 4.5% annual fees will only grow to $29,177.57.
- The passively managed portfolio with 0.03% annual fees grows to a whopping $66,909—more than twice the actively managed portfolio!

To build your wealth through investing, embrace low-cost index funds that are passively managed.

The Zen of Passive Investing: Simplicity Breeds Success

Successful Investing Principle 2: Harness the Power of Passive Investing

Passive investing means two things:

- You purchase index funds that are passively managed, which means they don't try to outperform the market but rather replicate the market.

- You refrain from personally, actively trading these funds to try and time the market.

Remember, no one knows what is going to happen in the short term. No one has a crystal ball. That's a myth.

As I mentioned before, actively managed investments underperform over the long term. Your best bet is to invest in passively managed funds that replicate the market without all the fees.

The Marathon Mindset: Embracing Long-Term Investing

Successful Investing Principle 3: Commit to the Long-Term Perspective

Investing is a slow way to become wealthy. It won't happen overnight, and along the way there will be ups and downs.

A lot of people get nervous about investing because of the potential to lose money. After all, what happens if another financial crash such as the 2008 financial crisis happens again?

From October 2007 to March 2009, the S&P 500 lost about 57% of its value. However, taking the long-term view, the returns from March 2009 to April 2021 were a whopping 494%!

Successful investors don't panic and sell at the sight of losses. Instead, they know that in the long term, the market recovers. In fact, when the market is declining is the perfect time to buy, because everything is cheaper.

This is also a good reason you shouldn't invest the money that you'll need in the next three to five years, as you could be forced to sell during a market decline. Instead, invest money for the long term with a long-term view.

The Patient Investor: Mastering the Buy and Hold Strategy

Successful Investing Principle 4: Master the Art of "Buy and Hold"

Every time you buy or sell, you will be facing costs. There are transaction costs that your brokerage or funds will be charging. Depending upon the type of account you are investing in, you may also have to pay short-term taxes. As we've talked about, all those costs can add up to be a substantial drag on the performance of your investments.

Additionally, many people will try to time the market. They think the market is going to go down, so they decide to sell to avoid the market decline.

However, as I mentioned before, no one knows what is going to happen in the short term. Trying to time the market most often results in investors missing out on some of the best performing days as a result.

Multiple studies have been conducted around this, but the most famous finding is this[9]:

- If you stayed invested completely in the S&P 500, your returns would be around 10%.[10]
- If you missed 10 of the best days because you were focused on "timing," then your returns would drop to 5%!

The difference is stark. Don't play the game of trying to time the market. Instead, buy and hold for the long run.

Diversification: Your Financial Safety Net

Successful Investing Principle 5: Diversify Wisely

Buying individual stocks is risky. Yes, you can get higher returns, but this comes with the increased risk of larger declines.

---

9 Fidelity Investments. (2023). The impact of missing the best days in the market. Retrieved from https://www.fidelity.com/bin-public/060_www_fidelity_com/documents/dont-miss-best-days.pdf

10 The S&P 500 is a stock market index that tracks the performance of 500 of the largest publicly traded companies in the United States, representing a broad measure of the U.S. equity market.

It is hard (impossible, really) to pick the winners and losers. Additionally, when it comes to individual companies, some of them can decline to $0, wiping out your entire investment, because of mismanagement, fraud, and/or bankruptcy.

As a cautionary tale, recall these companies that were once "high flyers" and considered invincible:

- **Enron Corporation:** Once a giant in the energy sector, Enron's stock price collapsed in 2001 following revelations of widespread accounting fraud. This scandal not only led to the bankruptcy of the company but also resulted in significant regulatory changes in the form of the Sarbanes-Oxley Act.

- **Lehman Brothers Holdings Inc.:** A global financial services firm, Lehman Brothers filed for bankruptcy in 2008 amidst the subprime mortgage crisis, marking the largest bankruptcy filing in U.S. history at the time. Its failure was a pivotal moment in the global financial crisis, leading to a severe contraction in the world's financial markets.

- **WorldCom:** In 2002, WorldCom, a telecommunications company, was involved in a massive accounting scandal that led to its bankruptcy. The company had inflated its assets by as much as $11 billion, which at the time was the largest accounting fraud in history.

- **Blockbuster LLC:** Once the dominant movie rental service, Blockbuster filed for bankruptcy in 2010, unable to adapt to the changing market and the rise of digital streaming platforms like Netflix. Its stock value plummeted as it failed to pivot its business model effectively.

- **Toys "R" Us:** The iconic toy retailer filed for bankruptcy in 2017 after struggling with a heavy debt load and intense competition from online retailers. Although it attempted a comeback, the original company's equity value essentially went to zero.

- **Theranos:** Theranos, a health technology company, became infamous for its false claims about revolutionizing blood testing. The company dissolved in 2018 amid mounting legal challenges and scandals, with its stock becoming worthless.

The adage of "don't put all your eggs in one basket" applies to investing. Instead of buying single stocks, it is better to purchase index funds that go out and buy hundreds or even thousands of stocks. This diversifies your risk and gives you exposure to the broad market, while protecting you from the danger of being exposed to any one single stock. If you've bought thousands of stocks and one of them ends up going down significantly (or even going bankrupt), then the impact to you will be minimal, since it represents such a small fraction of your overall investment portfolio.

In the words of John C. Bogle, Founder of Vanguard Group: "Don't look for the needle in the haystack. Just buy the haystack!"

From Theory to Practice: Kickstarting Your Investment Journey

Now, let's pull everything together in terms of how to prioritize your investing in different accounts.

1. Contribute to your 401(k) or 403(b) up to the match amount to take advantage of the full match offered by your employer (e.g. if your employer offers to match up to 5% of your salary, then contribute 5% and you'll get a 5% match from them).
2. If you still have non-mortgage debt (e.g. student loans, cars, etc.) then prioritize paying off your debt.
3. After your non-mortgage debt is paid off, maximize your contribution to your 401(k) or 403(b) to take advantage of reducing your taxable income while investing in a tax-deferred account.
4. After you maximize your 401(k)/403(b) contribution, invest in an HSA if you are eligible for one..
5. After maximizing an HSA, maximize a Roth IRA using after tax money.
6. After maximizing a Roth IRA, then open a taxable brokerage account and invest the remaining money you have to invest.

The above approach to your accounts ensures you are taking advantage of a match, prioritizing paying off debt, and taking advantage of the tax benefits that the various accounts offer. Notice that investing in a taxable brokerage account happens last, due to the fact that this account has none of the tax benefits the other accounts offer.

As we've discussed before, after you pay off your non-mortgage debt, you should be aiming to save and invest at least 20% of your income. However, you can significantly increase this savings and investing amount, which will accelerate reaching financial freedom.

For instance, if you have a spouse or partner and each of you make the same amount, then could you live on one income and save the other income? Doing that will put your savings and investing rate to 50% and will dramatically speed things up.

In fact, one of the biggest variables toward your financial freedom is your saving and investing rate. To illustrate this, let's assume you earn $100,000/year. Here is how long it takes for your portfolio to reach $1 million given different investing percentages (assuming 10% annual returns):

- If you invest 5% yearly, it will take about 32 years to become a millionaire.
- If you invest 10% yearly, it will take about 25 years to become a millionaire.
- If you invest 20% yearly, it will take about 19 years to become a millionaire.

- If you invest 30% yearly, it will take about 15 years to become a millionaire.
- If you invest 50% yearly, it will take about 12 years to become a millionaire.

What does the above illustrate? Well, many times I've found one of two things occurring:

- OTs are dramatically under-saving and under-investing. They haven't yet taken personal finance seriously and run the numbers, and so they think they are on track by investing 3% a year. Unfortunately, at that rate you'll have to work forever.
- They don't realize that they have permission to increase their savings and investing rate. They get anchored to a certain number and never realize that it is entirely up to them to increase it. If you saved 10% last year, what do you need to do next year to save 15%? Or could you simplify things and save 30%? It is fully up to you. The more you save and invest the faster you'll reach financial freedom.

An example I love to use often is to imagine an OT and a PT are married (this is pretty common!). Let's say both make $85k/year for a household income of $170,000. Ask yourself, could you live on one income and save the other one?

Now, before you break out a pen and paper to write me hate mail about how hard it is to save, let me gently remind you that the average *household* income in 2022 was $74,580. Not per person, per household! So what I'm saying is: could you find a way to live like an average American? All those other households have had to live on $74,580 out of necessity. Could you find a way to live on $85,000/year out of choice while saving the other salary? It is absolutely possible. It isn't necessarily easy, but your level of desire for financial freedom will dictate the level of sacrifice you are willing to make.

How would this exactly work in this example? Here's how to do it:

- We first imagine that the other salary doesn't exist. We pretend that one person isn't working, so they have to live on one salary of $85,000.
- If they only had one salary of $85,000, then their annual take home pay (after taxes, deductions, etc.) would equate to about $72,000 per year. They can spend $72,000 per year.
- Next, we go back to the fact that they make $170,000/year, and we figure out how to maximize their savings and investing to such an extent that, at the end, they still have $72,000 per year to spend.
- In 2025, the 401(k) contribution limit per individual was $23,500. Remember, contributing to a 401(k) is done using pre-tax money, so you'll actually reduce your taxable income.

- Both spouses maximize their 401(k) contribution. This is $47,000 being saved each year (pre-tax).
- Each employer matches the 401(k) contribution up to 5%. This is another $4,250 per person or another $8,500 per couple.
- The couple's taxable income will be $123,000 ($170,000 - $47,000 in pre-tax 401(k) contributions).
- The after-tax take home pay on $123,000 for a family of four is approximately $100,000.
- This means there is another $28,000 ($100,000 in take-home pay versus spending $72,000/year) of savings and investing they can do.
- So, let's add everything up. They contribute $47,000 in pre-tax money. They receive $8,500 in 401(k) matches. And they invest $28,000 in after-tax money (in Roth IRAs, etc.). In total, they are investing $83,500/year and still are living on $72,000/year. This is incredible. They are able to do this because they minimize their taxes by investing pre-tax money and take advantage of the employer match of their 401(k).

If they save and invest $83,500/year at a 10% yearly return, then this couple will be - millionaires in eight years!

Empowering OTs to Invest with Confidence

Let's wrap up this chapter with a bang! We've covered a ton of ground here, from the nitty-gritty of assets and accounts to busting those pesky investment myths that hold so many people back. By now, you've got a solid grasp on what it takes to invest like a pro and build that financial freedom that every OT deserves.

Here's the deal: successful investing boils down to a few key principles. Keep your costs low, embrace the power of passive investing, spread your money around (a.k.a. diversify!), and master the art of buying and holding. Simple, right? Here's the thing—simple doesn't mean easy. It takes discipline, patience, and a willingness to stick to your guns when the market gets a little crazy.

If there's one thing I know about OTs, it's that you've got the skills, the smarts, and the determination to make this investing thing work for you. So, take a deep breath, trust in the process, and remember that every journey starts with a single step. Whether you're starting out with your employer-sponsored plan or ready to dive into the world of IRAs and taxable accounts, the key is to get started. Trust me, your future self will thank you.

CHAPTER NINE

INCREASE YOUR INCOME AND PERSONAL SATISFACTION WITH "THE SWEET SPOT PRACTICE"

"The best way to predict your future is to create it."

– Abraham Lincoln

So far, we've covered how to create a conscious spending plan, how to reduce your debt, and how to save and invest your hard-earned OT money.

For many, you could stop right here and be on the path to financial freedom and flexibility. However, let's be frank for a second.

The Undeniable Truth: OTs are Vastly Underpaid

OTs are significantly underpaid on average. You are underpaid compared to your level of education, your level of student loan debt, your level of commitment to your clients, and the impact you have on your clients' lives.

At the same time, more and more OTs are finding themselves stuck in jobs that demand high productivity standards with stagnant growth in their income. Add on onerous documentation requirements, and it is no wonder that OTs burn out.

However, there is a way you to:

- See as many or as few clients as you'd like each day
- Not spend so much time on documentation
- Pick what days of the week you'd like to work to fit your life
- Increase your income
- Work with highly motivated clients who light you up during each session

And the way to do this is with what I call the "Sweet Spot Practice."

Introducing the Sweet Spot Practice: Your Key to Balance and Prosperity

A Sweet Spot Practice is a practice where you:

- Decide on who your ideal clients are
- Determine your fee per hour

- Set a schedule that supports your income goals + lifestyle goals
- Get amazing results for highly motivated clients

This isn't a pipe dream. It is something that entrepreneurial-minded OTs are living each day.

My OT students, like Isabel Hartounian of Thrive Maternal, are doing it. She is a pelvic floor therapist who primarily sees pre/postnatal women. She works four days/week in her own practice and each week enjoys a three-day weekend (the third day is spent catching up on business tasks and prioritizing self-care).

Here's the kicker: she only sees three clients/day and at the time of this writing has a six-week waitlist. She charges $200/session, so each week she brings in $2,400, or $9,600/month. Over a yearly basis, this would be revenue of $115k/year.

Not too bad for only seeing three clients/day for four days a week. And, at the time of this book's publication, she was in the process of hiring another OT to work in her practice. She's got ample time for her clients, for follow-ups, for taking care of herself, and for being present with her family. Her life feels expansive.

Isabel could see more clients each week (after all, she has a six-week waitlist) and make even more money. But, she likes the lifestyle balance she has currently. She earns good money, gets clients great results, and isn't exhausted at the end of the day, so she can show up fully in the other roles she has.

Contrast that with the typical OT who is seeing 10-15 clients/day—not each week! It is no wonder so many OTs are burning out and struggling financially.

So, how are OTs like Isabel reclaiming treatment freedom, money freedom and time freedom?

Breaking Free from Insurance Constraints

OTs like Isabel can find a better balance for one central reason: *They don't take insurance.*

See, many of the current problems OTs face in their working life come down to the simple fact that they work within an insurance-based world. When you are in-network for insurance, it creates a ton of incentives (and not the right ones) that many OTs don't realize:

1. A third party that isn't in the treatment room now dictates reimbursement rates (hint: these reimbursement rates typically go down over time; while increases can happen, they are rare).
2. Those reimbursement rates directly correlate to how much your employer can pay you (after all, a business can't pay you money that it doesn't have).

3. Reimbursement rates going down creates a perverse business incentive for OTs to see as many clients each day to maximize billings.
4. So, talented OTs like you get stuck in the middle having to work more and more for less and less. It is a cycle that keeps more and more OTs stuck and burning out.
5. Plus. . . clients may not like the care they receive as just a number in a big system.

Here's another sobering fact: Insurance companies reimburse the same rate per CPT code regardless of whether the service was performed by an OT with one year of experience or fifteen years of experience.

This leads to a tremendous amount of frustration for OTs who have dedicated their careers and their weekends (pursuing continuing education) and yet don't see salary growth.

As OTs, it is normal and acceptable to want to see growth: growth in your skills, growth in your client results, and yes, growth in your financial compensation as you become more and more skilled.

But, OTs will always be capped and underearn what they should be making by being in the insurance world. It is a fact—it is the way the system works, and it won't be changing anytime soon.

However, with private pay, you don't have to limit yourself as an OT. The greatest gift to your client and yourself is to treat:

- *Who* you want
- *When* you want
- *Where* you want
- *How* you want
- And for as *long* as you want

That is true freedom. That's Freedom of Practice, and that's what's possible when you step outside of insurance and become private pay.

You Deserve It and Your Clients Will Thank You

When my wife and I started our OT private pay practice (called The Functional Pelvis) in NYC back in 2014, it was the best decision we ever made. At the time, my wife and I had a two-year-old at home and had just welcomed our second. Six weeks after my wife gave birth to our son, we filed the incorporation paperwork.

Some would say we were crazy to tackle this much at the same time, but we knew we had to do it. Working in a hospital while pregnant was enough for my wife to realize that she couldn't do that for the rest of her career.

With two young kiddos, most people would (understandably) hold steady and delay taking a risk. But it was exactly because we had two young children that we felt a strong need to *take* a risk. Why? Because we wanted so badly what was on the other side of that risk.

After the experience of working in a hospital, she knew that a traditional OT role would be at odds with being a parent, a spouse, and an individual. She wanted to be able to easily take a Friday off to be a chaperone at our kid's school. She wanted to work with highly motivated clients who she could see for extended periods of time (90 minute evals + 60 minute treatments). After all, that was why she became an OT. The joy of being an OT arose through developing deep bonds with her clients, problem-solving with them, and seeing them progress.

She didn't want to come home exhausted at the end of each day. She wanted to specialize and work within her zone of genius without all of the additional barriers that insurance puts up. In short: she wanted to be the OT she went to school to be. She wanted to focus on the quality of care—not the quantity of clients. So, we filed the paperwork to incorporate and have never looked back.

Opening our private pay practice forced us to confront a lot of emotions and worries:

- Were we making our services inaccessible by sticking to private pay?

- Would people really come to us if we didn't accept insurance?
- We'd never opened a business before—who the heck were we to think we could?

These are the exact same worries shared by most of my OT students in my program, "Private Pay MBA." And they are valid concerns. But these thoughts are often not examined in more detail to understand exactly their implications. So, let's dig into these in more detail to see if a.) they are true and b.) if they are serving you.

Serving with Intention: Overcoming Guilt and Defining Your Impact

First, I'll say that there is a lot of unfair judgement and guilt around making money in healthcare. This is perpetuated by companies (and some individual therapists) that take advantage of your people-pleasing tendencies by making you feel bad for wanting to earn a decent living while not burning yourself out.

The truth is that you will be a better OT and get better results for your clients if you are operating from a place of abundance. Abundance of time. Abundance of wealth—however you define that. And abundance of options. You'll be a better OT if you are making a healthy living that allows you to have adequate time for your clients without experiencing chronic stress about money and burning out.

If you earn a good living, you'll also be able to afford to offer pro-bono work or sliding scale work. When you earn more money and free up your time, you can be intentional on how you give back.

Let's cover a frank truth: it is literally impossible for everyone to be your client. I know we say things like "I want to serve everyone," but that's a physically impossible goal. There is no way you can possibly serve everyone. So, the question becomes: How can you have the most impact in your community?

You have constraints, including time, energy, and money. We need to be honest about this. You can't do everything and be everything to everyone. This is super important and a source of a lot of guilt, shame, and anger in healthcare.

I'll repeat it again: you can't do everything and be everything to everyone. And that is okay. Coming to terms with this allows us to move to the next step, which is: "With my constraints, with my desire to protect my physical and mental health, how can I have the most impact within my community?"

Frankly, a private pay practice is one of the only things that you can do that protects your mental and physical well-being while giving you plenty of options to give back to your community. With a private pay practice, you can earn a full-time living working three days/week, do pro-bono work on the fourth day and have a three-day weekend each week so you can rest and recharge.

You can work from a place of excitement and opportunity, rather than from a place of shame, guilt and resentment. Which sounds better to you?

For us, we started with all those fears and doubts, but they quickly dissipated as we attracted and worked with highly motivated clients. When we found the right clients, not only did they not mind paying cash, but they were so invested in their own healthcare that they sang our praises to their friends and family. The best indication that we were on the right path was the feedback we got from our clients.

That was true for us, it has been true for my students, and I think you'll find it to be true for yourself.

Ideal Clients Are Willing to Invest in Results

It is natural to get worried about clients not being willing to pay out of pocket for your services. I have two reminders for you:

1. You need a lot fewer people than you think paying out of pocket to replace your full-time income or you could just see clients "on the side" to add extra income.

2. Many other professions don't accept insurance, charge full fees, and are booked solid.

See, when you only work in an insurance-based environment, it is easy to fall into the trap that insurance is the most important thing. You constantly hear things like:

- "Insurance won't cover this service."
- "Another claim got denied, we need to adjust the documentation and resubmit."
- "We can't proceed until we verify your insurance coverage."
- "Insurance capped the number of sessions we can provide."
- "Insurance doesn't cover that specific intervention, so we need to find an alternative."

Insurance isn't the same as healthcare. And insurance isn't the most important thing to many clients. At the end of the day, clients don't want sessions—they want results. They want to meet their goals faster and more completely.

If you can see them for 60-minute sessions where you are solely dedicated to their care, then many clients will be perfectly comfortable submitting your services to their insurance company under their out-of-network benefits.

Let's assume you'd like to earn $100k annually (before expenses/taxes) and you charge $125/hr. Let's say your average plan of care is six visits. Then, this means you need only 133 clients per year. That's probably a lot less people than you realize.

Those same 133 people are also currently paying out of pocket for things like orthodontics, dentists, chiropractors, massage therapy, personal training, psychologist, car repairs, installing a new A/C in their house, and replacing their roof. What these people are willing to invest in isn't about the service itself—it's about the solution. If you can show them that your expertise will help them meet their goals faster and more effectively, they'll see your care as a worthy investment, just like they do with other professionals who provide value.

The bottom line? Your ideal clients are out there, ready and willing to invest in themselves. It's your job to show them how your services can help them achieve the results they want.

Supercharging Your Retirement: The Owner's Advantage

I'm not going to mince words here: The US tax code is set up to benefit owners much more than employees.

Talking about taxes is about as much fun as getting a root canal. And if you really wanted to nerd out on the deep, dense tax code, you could spend years and years doing so (at great cost to your social life). The vast majority of us won't do that, though, so I'm going to give you the two most significant advantages from a tax perspective for owners:

1. You get to deduct a lot more things inside your business
2. You can supercharge your retirement savings

Let's take #1 first. Inside your practice, you can deduct all sorts of things you are probably already paying for without the tax benefit:

- Cell phone
- Continuing education
- Supplies
- Health insurance premiums
- Meals and conference travel
- Mileage and expenses with your vehicle for work purposes

Of course, you'll want to work with a qualified accountant to make sure that each and everything you deduct is appropriate and justifiable. There is tremendous opportunity to deduct a wide variety of expenses within your practice that you likely are already incurring.

Next comes retirement savings, which is where you can supercharge things.

We've discussed the 401(k) in earlier chapters, so you are already familiar with how your contributions reduce your taxable income. Well, as a practice owner you can set up a

401(k) program for your practice. If you don't plan on having any employees (aside from your spouse), this is called a Solo 401(k) or sometimes referred to as Individual 401(k) or Self-Employed 401(k). These are easy to set up with brokerage companies like Vanguard or Fidelity.

Now, here's the kicker: The Solo 401(k) supercharges your retirement savings. As an employee, you can contribute $23,500 (as of 2025) of your salary pre-tax to the Solo 401(k). As the owner, and this is where it gets interesting, you can MATCH your salary at 25%! This is huge. Most employers match anywhere from 3% to 7% if you are lucky.

According to the actual rules, the employer (you) can match 25%. The employer + employee contributions must be below $66,000 in 2025 or $73,500 if you are older than 50. Think about it: Where else do you have the potential to save $66,000/year tax free?

Let's say you are a solo-practice owner with $150,000 of revenue after expenses. You've set up a Solo 401(k), a retirement plan that allows you to save as both an employee and an employer. Here's how you can take advantage of it while keeping things simple.

Step 1: Pay Yourself a Salary

Out of the $150,000, you decide to pay yourself a salary of $106,914. This is the amount you'll use to calculate both your retirement contributions and payroll taxes.

Step 2: Maximize Your Retirement Contributions

As the employee, you can contribute up to $23,500 of your salary to your Solo 401(k). This reduces your taxable income and allows you to save for retirement. As the employer, you can contribute an additional 25% of your salary, which amounts to $26,728. This is a business expense, further lowering your taxable income. Altogether, you've set aside $50,228 for retirement in one year!

Step 3: Cover Payroll Taxes

As the business owner, you're responsible for paying payroll taxes—15.3% of your salary for Social Security and Medicare. On a salary of $106,914, that comes to $16,358.

Step 4: Where Does the $150,000 Go?

Here's how your revenue is allocated:

1. Your Salary: $106,914 (what you pay yourself)
2. Employer Retirement Contribution: $26,728 (25% of your salary to your Solo 401(k))
3. Payroll Taxes: $16,358 (to cover Social Security and Medicare)

At the end of the day, you've used the full $150,000 of revenue to:

- Pay yourself a reasonable salary

- Maximize your retirement savings
- Cover your tax obligations

So, to recap, what's happened here:

- You pay yourself a salary of $106,914. You contribute $23,500 to your Solo 401(k), which reduces the taxes you personally pay on your salary, as you only pay taxes on $83,414 ($106,914 - $23,500).
- Your business contributes $26,728 to your 401(k), which means you are saving a grand total of $50,228 tax free which you invest in low-cost index funds like we've discussed.
- Out of the $150,000, you've saved $50,228 toward retirement, paid yourself $83,414, and paid payroll taxes of $16,358.
- You've saved on taxes personally (through your 401(k) contribution), and your business saves on taxes from its contribution match.

Imagine how quickly you can reach your financial goals by investing $50,228 each year toward retirement while still paying yourself a great salary? If you do that for 11 years and earn a 10% annual return, you'll become a millionaire.

Now, here's the big question. . . is it actually possible to have $150,000 of revenue net of your expenses in a private pay practice? Surely it must require you to still see 10 to 15 clients a day and have no social life. Right?

Wrong. Let's do a quick calculation:

- You see five clients/day and you work four days/week.
- That's 20 client visits per week.
- You charge $200/visit (yes, people will pay this).
- You take four weeks of vacation each year, so you are only working 48 weeks/year.
- Well, 48 weeks x 20 clients/week x $200/client = $192,000 a year.
- Now, let's factor in a 10% no show and cancellation rate, so you actually have revenue of $172,800.
- That leads you to be able to have fixed expenses of $22,800/year and have $150,000 available to pay yourself and contribute to your 401(k).

Of course, your situation and goals will be different. So, view this as more of an accordion where things move and aren't static. You could adjust your pricing up or down, leading to bigger or smaller revenue. You could adjust the number of clients you see a day or the number of days you work. You could also decide not to match a full 25% but still do a great match of 15%, which would enable you to pay yourself more.

Crunching the Numbers: Employees vs. Practice Owners

To bring this home even more, let's compare what we've seen in this chapter to the typical OT who is working for someone else and making $75,000/year but maximizing their 401(k) contribution:

	Solo Practice Owner	OT Employee	Calculation Notes
Salary	$106,914	$75,000	A
401(k) contribution (employee)	$23,500	$23,500	B
401(k) match from employer	$26,728.50	$3,750.00	C (= 25% x A for owner, 5% x A for employee)
Total 401(k) savings	$50,228.50	$27,250.00	B + C
Taxable income	$83,414	$51,500	A - B
After-tax pay (approximate)	$63,707	$40,652	

As you can see, the solo practice owner earns almost 50% more in after-tax pay ($64k vs $41k) *and* saves almost 100% more for retirement ($50k vs $27k) compared to the OT employee.

And... the solo practice owner achieves this with only working four days/week and seeing five clients/day compared to the OT employee seeing 10 to 15 clients/day.

So, the big question is: which life do you want? Which life makes you feel empowered and allows you to show up the best? Which life are you striving toward?

Of course, opening an OT private pay practice involves risk, including the risk that it won't be successful. The flip side is that staying an OT employee also carries with it significant risks that we don't normally consider:

- The risk of getting fired;
- The great health risk (physical and mental) from experiencing burnout;
- The great financial risk of missing out on salary increases and bigger retirement contributions.

Sweet Spot Practices are Surprisingly Easy to Start

I'm always amazed that entrepreneurship isn't taught more in OT school.

Did you know that 80% of dentists work for themselves? Think about that for a second: in dental school you've got 8 out of 10 people in a classroom looking around going: "One day I'm going to own my own practice—why would I work for someone else?" and then they do it!

And starting a dental practice isn't easy or cheap. Before you even open the doors and collect your first cleaning fee you've got to:

- Sign a lease and spend hundreds of thousands of dollars renovating the space
- Spend hundreds of thousands of dollars on dental equipment
- Hire front office staff and dental hygienists

It is easy to spend $750,000 to a million to open the practice. And this is on top of the hundreds of thousands of dollars the dentist has in student loans.

Opening an OT private pay practice is a walk in the park compared to a dentistry practice and doesn't cost a ton of money.

So, what do you need to start a private pay practice? There are a few important steps:

- Incorporate your practice—this protects you. You can do this for a few hundred dollars or pay an online service to do it for you.

- Purchase liability insurance to make sure you are protected.
- Decide where you'll see clients. You've got four different options. You could do mobile, rent a room (from another practice that isn't using it), lease an entire space (the most expensive) or do virtual.

You can get started for less than $1,000.

Are there other things that you should do and spend your money on to make it successful? Yes. I'm being a bit extreme on purpose, because we tend to make it too complicated. There isn't a huge barrier to you seeing private clients in the next few weeks.

Most of the barriers to seeing clients privately actually have more to do with our mindset than any real barriers. That's why in my mentoring and coaching program, Private Pay MBA, we spend the entire first chapter on mindset, and it also comes up in my weekly coaching calls with OTs.

The Main Limiting Belief Holding OTs Back From Starting Private Pay Practices

Honestly, this section could be expanded to seven different limiting beliefs. Indeed, there is typically this collection of things like imposter feelings, lack of time, etc. all happening at the same time. It is about as clear as a muddy lake and leads to a lot of analysis paralysis and second guessing.

I want to address the elephant in the room and a comment that's made frequently: "Doug, I didn't get into OT to only serve the rich, and I don't want to limit access."

I fully understand and sympathize with this well-meaning sentiment. And we used to feel the same way until we realized a few important things.

This statement rarely gets closely examined, and it makes everyone seem altruistic, so it is tough to take an opposing position. After all, if you disagree with this statement, then surely you must be for limiting access, right?

Well, no, actually.

Let's examine the last part of the statement more closely, honing in on "I don't want to limit access" and really breaking this down. I'd like to illustrate this with a story that AOTA President Alyson Stover told me when I interviewed her on my YouTube channel. You can find the entire interview on YouTube by searching "The Future of Occupational Therapy is Entrepreneurship with Alyson Stover."

Alyson, a pediatric OT, was telling her friend about a new Medicare rule that said only Orthotists could be reimbursed for splints. At the time, Alyson was seeing a lot of kids with Medicaid, and Medicaid followed what Medicare would reimburse for, so Alyson wasn't getting reimbursed.

Alyson was sharing this with her friend and describing how she would go and fabricate the splint, the orthotist would get reimbursed, and everyone would pat Alyson on the back and say something like: "Wow, the dedication and commitment you have to this is incredible."

And that is when Alyson's friend looked at her and said, "I actually think you are terrible as an occupational therapist." (I'm not joking. . . go look at my full interview with her. This story starts at 22:40.) Alyson was absolutely flabbergasted. Didn't her friend hear just how much she was doing? And then her friend said:

> *You're doing your entire profession a disservice, because I don't have the skill to sit down and make a splint. And the fact that you do and that you can do it with a child and that you can do it with a child who's squirming and has no attention and doesn't even want to be there is actually really complex.*
>
> *And every time you do that for free, you tell the world, 'oh, it's not hard.' See, when you do that, you reduce the reimbursement, you reduce the payment and the opportunity for people to place a value on your work.*
>
> *And when you do that, that means that your profession will continuously get paid less, because every time it's evaluated what the cost or value of your services and skills*

are, they're going to decrease because they didn't have to pay for it here, but it still got done. And then when it pays less, people can't enter your field. And if people can't enter your field, guess what? You've actually eliminated access across the nation.

So, really, by not valuing yourself and requiring adequate payment and reimbursement for your services, it might take a little longer, but you're actually going to minimize access because you're going to decrease the reimbursement, which will essentially become a barrier for entry into the field.

I was blown away by this when Alyson and I were talking. It is absolutely true. If you don't place value on the work you do, if you continue to accept less and less for your amazing skills, then you are actually eliminating access, because it reduces incentives and increases barriers for new OTs to enter the field.

And so we have to flip the script. You aren't eliminating access. You are actually ensuring that, as a profession, occupational therapy continues to be an amazing career that OTs can actually afford to practice in.

This leads me to the second point. When you adequately charge what you are worth, you suddenly have both the money *and* time to give back in meaningful ways.

Alyson has many therapists working for her at her clinic, Capable Kids, in Hermitage, Pennsylvania. She went on to describe how she still carries a small caseload in her clinic. But guess what? For her personal caseload, she doesn't charge for her services. She provides them pro bono to people who would not otherwise have had access to services.

It reminds me of a student of mine named Chelsea. Chelsea was worried about access as well. She felt conflicted between her personal roles and her professional role. She wanted to "give back" but also have a work schedule and life that didn't burn her out and aligned with her values.

And so, Chelsea sees 18 clients a week. She charges cash for her sessions and gives her clients superbills for them to submit to their insurance company for reimbursement according to their out-of-network benefits.

She works only four days a week in her practice, seeing four to five clients/day. Her husband drops their kids off at school each morning and Chelsea ends her day in time for her to pick up her kids. She coaches her oldest daughter's soccer team, so a few days each week her afternoons are filled with practices and time with her daughter.

Giving back is important to her, so on the fifth day she does pro bono work in a lower-income neighboring town. She sees between four and six clients and doesn't charge them a penny. And she isn't conflicted about taking care of others, because she has set up her life to be able to take care of herself and her family while still giving back.

She and her husband rescued a bulldog and fell in love with the breed. Local rescue organizations run on volunteers and donations. Not only do they volunteer on the weekend, but they regularly donate to the organization to help cover medical bills, boarding and food.

Chelsea is having an impact with her time through pro bono work and volunteering, as well as her money through charitable giving.

Lastly, it isn't just the rich that go to private pay practices. The types of clients you'll attract in a private pay practice are those that are highly motivated and prioritize their health. They are looking for expert care where they feel seen and heard as a client. They want one-on-one care (often 60-minute or 90-minute appointments) with a dedicated OT. They don't want to sign up for sessions—they want transformation and results as fast as possible.

The Five Must-Haves When Starting a Private Pay Practice

Unfortunately, because the barrier to start seeing clients privately is so low, I do see many OTs starting their practices without understanding the business aspect. After helping hundreds of OTs start their practice, I'd like to share some nonnegotiables to keep in mind, if you are considering starting your own practice. These will help you avoid these common mistakes, setting yourself up for success.

Here are the five must-haves:

1. Have a specialty
2. Have a marketing plan and budget
3. Know your numbers
4. Build relationships
5. Get help

Let's take these one by one.

Have a Specialty

Having a specialty is critical for any OT who is looking at seeing clients privately, either full-time or on the side.

Our specialty was pelvic floor therapy. We weren't providing general OT services. With pelvic floor therapy, we were solving a specific problem and meeting a need.

Yours could be hands, low-vision, neuro, pediatrics, feeding, etc. Whatever it is, you need a specialty to attract private pay clients. Why? Well, the clients you want to attract have specific problems and want specific results. And having a specialty allows you to further refine it into a niche.

What's a niche? A niche is a specific population with a specific problem that you are uniquely suited to help. It is all about narrowing your focus so you can serve a specific audience instead of trying to appeal to everyone.

To give an example from our practice. Our specific niche was not only pelvic floor therapy, but pelvic floor therapy for new moms. We could have seen a wide range of clients, but we determined that to be the population we wanted to work with the most.

The result? All our marketing language was geared toward new moms. When new moms landed on our website or saw our marketing materials, they immediately felt understood and that we were the #1 solution for them.

Have a Marketing Plan and Budget

I know we've all heard the adage: "If you build it, they will come." In private practice, it is much more like: "If you build it, be prepared to talk about it endlessly, and then they'll come."

Talking endlessly about it requires both a marketing plan and a budget. Unfortunately, this is where most OTs get stuck. They've technically opened a practice (remember that the barriers aren't high), but they don't have clients.

Many OTs fear marketing and putting themselves out there. But marketing doesn't have to be a four-letter word. You can market yourself authentically and ethically.

You change people's lives. Why not share that? How happy would you be to take a nice long gulp of ice-cold water after walking in the desert for two days? You'd feel amazing!

And guess what, when your ideal client hears about your services, you are the proverbial ice-cold water to them. They've likely been suffering with their problem for some time. They've probably tried lots of different things without results. You and your practice are a source of hope and solution to them—not a bother. The right client wants exactly what you are offering. And developing a marketing plan and allocating a budget to it allows you to reach those right clients.

Most of the work I do with OTs in Private Pay MBA is around developing these marketing plans to start attracting their ideal clients.

Know Your Numbers

There are a few things you need to know from a numbers perspective:

1. KPIs (key performance indicators) for your practice
2. Your financial numbers

I like to tell my students to focus on three KPIs when they are starting:

1. How many inquiries are you getting?
2. How many of those inquiries turn into clients?
3. The average plan of care (POC) for your clients

If you don't have a full caseload, then these numbers will help you pinpoint where the problem lies. Are you getting lots of inquiries but not a lot of bookings? Well, you don't have a marketing problem. You either have a problem with where the leads are coming from, or you need to adjust how you talk to prospective clients on the phone.

If #1 and #2 are firing on all cylinders but you still aren't fully booked, then you likely have a problem with client retention. Instead of staying for six POC visits, they might be staying for only two visits. This means you need three times the leads compared to if they were staying for a full POC.

Next, you need to know your financial numbers so you can adequately know what to pay yourself. I would advise you to hire a great CPA and bookkeeper to help you track all of this. You need to know the basics, but you don't have to do everything yourself when there are talented professionals whose specialties lie in those areas. You'll sleep a lot better at night.

Build Relationships

You know the saying that real estate is all about location, location, location?

Well, in a private pay practice, your success is largely going to depend upon relationships, relationships, relationships.

Really, I can't emphasize this enough. Your network (e.g. your relationships) will be your net worth, as they say.

There is a lot of behind-the-scenes activity necessary to start a practice: reading your state practice act, filing for your legal entity, creating marketing materials, etc. These are all important.

However, the primary way to get clients through your door is to leave your office (or house!) and make connections in your community. Your ideal clients are already working with others in your community. They are already going to healthcare appointments, working out at gyms, doing hobbies, going to church, etc. Building relationships with those providers and professionals will supercharge your results.

A word of advice: expect to follow up and nurture these relationships. Provide value to them. Don't just ask for referrals. Relationships are fruitful and meaningful when both sides are helping the other to succeed. You want warm relationships, not transactional relationships. These take time and nurturing, so expect to follow up multiple times.

Get Help

A mentor will eliminate a lot of costly mistakes that OTs make when trying to do everything on their own. Getting a mentor is really about speed.

Yes, finding a mentor will likely cost you money, but it will also save you precious time, effort, and/or money.

In my course and mentorship program, Private Pay MBA, I teach OTs how to start thriving private pay practices. The OTs who join are an interesting mix. About 60% of the OTs are totally new to forming their practice. They might not even have a name picked out!

The other 40% are OTs who have been in practice for upwards of three years but tried to do it themselves. They've spent money on wasted efforts (e.g. buying doctors lunches) and spent years and countless sleepless nights trying to figure everything out themselves. They reached the conclusion that many other OTs have as well: it is better to spend a little bit of money now (which is tax deductible in your business) to get on solid ground.

After all—would you have tried to learn OT all by yourself? Or did you go to school, learn from professors, do fieldwork, etc.? Well, business is the same—that's why there is an entire MBA program at the graduate level. But you don't need an MBA to start your practice. You need the right business information distilled down and put concretely in terms of what it means to be an OT starting a private pay practice.

Of course, you don't have to work with me in Private Pay MBA, but I highly recommend you find someone qualified who not only has done it themselves (like we did with The Functional Pelvis), but has a track record of teaching other

OTs how to do it as well. Finding a mentor is all about making an investment with the expectation that you'll gain much more than its cost.

For instance, you might have sticker shock in joining a program that costs $2,000. But let's reframe this. Investing in your business shouldn't be a throw-away expense. You have to put the money in context of what you'll get and what it could return to you.

If you are charging $200/visit and the average plan of care is six visits, then each potential client is "worth" $1,200 to you. At $2,000, this means you'll only need to gain 1.6 clients to break even on the program.

So, ask yourself—can you learn something valuable (even if it is one small thing) that gets you 1.6 additional clients from what you learned? I would absolutely hope so!

And guess what? If you can get 16 clients using information from the program, then you have literally multiplied your investment by 10. Not only did you make your money back, but you increased it by a factor of 9 AND you learned business skills that will continue to generate new and returning clients. That is knowledge that is going to serve you for years to come and is, in my opinion, money well spent.

CHAPTER TEN

CONCLUSION

"Wealth isn't just about numbers; it's about freedom—freedom to live a life aligned with your values, your purpose, and your dreams."

– Doug Vestal, Ph.D.

Wow, this has been quite a wild ride. Congratulations on making it all the way to the end! We've covered everything from money trauma and debunking myths about the wealthy to how to pay off your student loans faster and the alphabet soup of investment accounts—and everything in between.

You now have all the knowledge you need to attain financial freedom as an OT. This book has given you the entire recipe to follow:

- Get on a conscious spending plan that aligns with your values
- Pay off your debt quickly
- Start investing right away and increase investments as you pay off your debt
- If needed, look for ways to increase your income

The hardest part lies in actually taking action and implementing the steps. As we talked about in the beginning of the book, the steps are simple, but that doesn't mean they are easy. It is often our own mindset and past money trauma that holds us back from implementing things. If you find yourself still stuck, go back to the earlier chapters and complete those exercises again.

Really start to tap into exactly why it is important for you to reach financial freedom:

- The ability to alleviate financial stress in your daily life
- The ability to pick where you work and with whom you work
- The ability to pick a work schedule that doesn't require you missing key events in your life
- The ability to have choices and live abundantly
- The ability to be independent and give back freely

There are literally hundreds of reasons why you might want to reach financial freedom. Focus on your big *why* and start taking the action steps I've laid out in this book.

When you experience a win on your journey toward financial freedom, take the time to celebrate it. Heck, even send me an email (seriously) at *dougvestal@freedomofpractice.com* and share your win with me. I'd love to share in celebrating your hard work and dedication.

ACKNOWLEDGEMENTS

When I had the idea of writing Financial Freedom for OTs, I had a strong desire to show OTs the tried-and-true ways to build financial freedom. I wanted it to be a resource for years to come that meets OTs where they are, gives them the just right challenge applied to their finances, and understands the unique challenges OTs face when it comes to personal finance.

Though I wrote each word on these pages, this book wouldn't be possible without an immense amount of support and encouragement.

I owe a deep gratitude to Lindsey, who is my amazing wife (and OT!). Lindsey - I wouldn't trade anything in the world for the life we've built together. The energy you bring into this world is infectious, you are an amazing mother, an amazing wife, and the strongest woman I know. With you, anything is possible.

To my two wonderful kids, Avery and Liam. You both are kind, hardworking, funny, and entrepreneurial. I love being your Dad and I'm so proud of you both. You two are the reasons your Mom and I live the way we do – we want to show you the great expansiveness that's possible in this world.

To my Mom and stepfather Frank: Thank you both for your unwavering love and support. You taught me how to stretch a dollar and always encouraged my interests and passions. This became rocket fuel for me.

To my two brothers David and Dennis. You both are amazing men. Somehow, all 3 of us got the gene to want to be dedicated Dads, great partners and good cooks.

This book wouldn't have seen the light of day if it wasn't for the incredible team at Novella Editorial. Nicole, you worked your proof-reading magic so that a reader could actually understand my thoughts. Ellie – you also worked your magic but most importantly, kept me and everyone on track so we could meet our deadlines. You kept the train moving smoothly and I'm impressed by your ability to juggle it all. Leonardo – people eat first with their eyes so thank you for the beautiful cover and interior design.

Lastly – a huge THANK YOU to all my OT supporters, students and readers. From speaking at the AOTA, to state conferences, to guest lectures at University's, to students in my courses and on social media – I've felt incredibly welcomed into this "second" career of mine. I'm incredibly inspired by the important work you do each day. You all are leaders and making a profound impact on the lives of your clients. I wrote this book in the hopes it will make a profound impact on your life in the same way you do for your clients.

Imagine Seeing 20 Clients/Week and Still Earning a Full-Time Income

I believe that OTs are at their best when you have occupational choice. I want you to have treatment freedom, time freedom and money freedom.

With a Private Pay OT Practice you can:

- Stop seeing 10 – 15 clients/day and instead see 15 – 20 clients/week
- Create a flexible schedule that works for you and your life
- Focus on building therapeutic rapport and treatment plans – not documentation

I've helped 100s of OTs start their Private Pay Practice either full-time or part-time through my course Private Pay MBA.

Checkout Private Pay MBA Today:

www.freedomofpractice.com/ppmba

ABOUT THE AUTHOR

Doug Vestal, Ph.D., helps OTs attain occupational choice and freedom by starting private pay practices. He co-founded The Functional Pelvis, a private pay OT practice with his OT wife, Lindsey. He has over 10 years' experience managing an OT private practice and has helped 100s of OTs start private pay practices. Before working with OTs he spent 15 years in senior management positions on Wall Street, including the Global Head of Counterparty Credit Risk at a major investment bank.

He loves combining his business acumen, passion for entrepreneurship, and his deep knowledge of OTs to help them find treatment, time and money freedom on their terms. He has a Master's in Financial Mathematics and a Ph.D. in Applied Probability.

Do you have any questions? Get in touch!

- www.freedomofpractice.com
- @vestaldoug
- @dougvestal

cover and interior designed by Novella Editorial

www.ingramcontent.com/pod-product-compliance
Lightning Source LLC
Chambersburg PA
CBHW020455030426
42337CB00011B/119